KU-191-105

WEB OF WORDS

Also by David Bodanis
THE SECRET HOUSE

Web of Words

The Ideas behind Politics

David Bodanis

MACMILLAN
PRESS

© David Bodanis 1988

All rights reserved. No reproduction, copy or transmission
of this publication may be made without written permission.

No paragraph of this publication may be reproduced, copied
or transmitted save with written permission or in accordance
with the provisions of the Copyright Act 1956 (as amended),
or under the terms of any licence permitting limited copying
issued by the Copyright Licensing Agency, 33–4 Alfred Place,
London WC1E 7DP.

Any person who does any unauthorised act in relation to
this publication may be liable to criminal prosecution and
civil claims for damages.

First published 1988

Published by
THE MACMILLAN PRESS LTD
Houndmills, Basingstoke, Hampshire RG21 2XS
and London
Companies and representatives
throughout the world

Filmsetting by Vantage Photosetting Co. Ltd
Eastleigh and London

Printed in Hong Kong

British Library Cataloguing in Publication Data
Bodanis, David
Web of words: the ideas behind politics.
1. Political science
I. Title
320'.01   JA71
ISBN   0–333–38975–1 (hardcover)
ISBN   0–333–38976–X (paperback)

To my mother and the memory of my father:
who gave me meaning, language, life

Contents

Introduction and acknowledgements   *1*

PROLOGUE

Web of Words   7

PART ONE: TWO THEMES

1   Socialism, Bacteria, and the Obsessions of Pasteur   15

2   Pasteur II: Hitler's Bacteria   33

3   Commandos from the Invisible World   39

PART TWO: IN AMERICA

4   Creating the *New York Times*   57

5   *New York Times II*: Mozart and Bruce   79

6   *New York Times III*: The American Executive   85

PART THREE: SOME HISTORY

7   Money and Personality   99

PART FOUR: CONSOLATIONS

8   A Quiet Afternoon   149

Introduction and
Acknowledgments

I got the idea for this book when I moved to London after a long period in an out-of-the-way little village in France. In the village everyone had been nosey, and the numbers were low enough that with a lot of diligent prying everyone could be watched almost all the time. But in London: I remember walking through a sports center my first day there, and being amazed that everyone stayed so neatly in order, even though most of them didn't know each other, and there were no central figures doing any prying.

There seemed to be invisible rules, patterns, which people in the city were willing to follow. No doubt it was happening in America, where I had grown up, and on the political level too. It would be immensely illuminating to pull these patterns out, and then use them to see clearly the bases of our personal thinking and even our political choices. But how?

My approach was to start by taking all the fancy tools I knew from logic and philosophy, and try to apply them to the real nitty-gritty of what people get interested in: television shows, astrology, exciting commandos, marriage, and, the subject of what became the longest chapter in the book, money, money, money. It might have been easier to stay on an abstract level, but how would you ever know if you were right if you did that? Also, I didn't just want to make fun of what other people think – that's a style of writing not too appealing to see – and so made a point of including plenty of subjects for which I personally cared too.

Gradually certain patterns did begin to come clear, and once that happened I was able to go on to try to work out what was going on in our psychology, or what had happened in our political history, to have made us accept these patterns rather than others. Indirectly there is an attempt to develop the tool of what might be called hierarchy or mimicry theory, which is the study of links between ideas or doings held on one level of understanding with those on another. It all took a lot of reading, but was a delightful few years.

How to write up the results? As a tool for social thought, ordinary English is much underrated. Enriched by a little Yiddish, for that language's justly lauded ability to reach the parts other languages can't, it is without peer. Only in a few cases where there were no well-known terms around did I coin my own, whence the Blobs, Tarzan *vs* the Time Capsule, and other occasional oddities the reader might notice in the text.

I also left out footnotes. To some extent this was to make life easy for the printers; mostly, though, it was because recent social theorists – with a few delightful exceptions, such as Gellner, or Lévi-Strauss – haven't, unfortunately, had sufficient insight to come up with results worth quoting. It was tempting to source some of the arguments I used in the classical philosophers, but that is not the fashion any more.

The book itself ended up arranged like one of those musical pieces that keeps on developing a theme until you've gone in a full spiral, and are then looking down on where you started. So I start with just a little prologue, ostensibly comparing British and American English, but really bringing in that main point about there being a lot of ideas surrounding us, which we take for granted but which are important in shaping the way we think. That alone is of course not original – Aristotle and the Old Testament went on at length about our being blinded by preconceptions – and what counts is the particular way it's worked out. The prologue hints at something of an explanation, but sticking to the tinkle tinkle of little British/American curios it doesn't get very far. That's easy on the reader; also when I wrote it – it originally appeared in *New Society* magazine and was the grounds for a kind Macmillan editor, Tim Farmiloe, commissioning the whole book – I didn't know any more.

The book proper begins with a section on what I think are two of the most important invisible backings to our thought around now. Here I really do take the time to go into their sources and recent history.

The first chapter looks at the notion of infection, which has much to do with worry about our own body and its breakdown. Curiously enough, some reading up on Pasteur showed that it also has long tied in with attitudes towards subversion and industrial workers. In the essay there are particular applications to recent foreign policy, including an explanation of why Reagan and other apparently decent Americans have become so unreasonable about the Sandinistas. To go with it there's a little follow-up essay applying the idea to the particular case of Hitler and the Jews. It's an important subject; also a way of checking our findings.

The second basic idea is the excitement with commandos, and hi-tech gear generally. Here I try to show that underlying this fascination is a worry about the basic question of how to act in life –

how to know what to do. To understand it you need to delve into Augustine and Homer; only after that, I think, does it become clear why even if we're against big defense budgets we are still, unfortunately, likely to get a special sort of excitement from thinking about Star Wars and similar weapons.

The next section, Part Two, tries to reveal how these and other ideas are at work in America today. It's always tempting to want to explain everything, but as that's the direction in which megalomania lies, I've stuck to just a few domains. The first chapter in the section, through a look at the *New York Times*, discusses the overall stability of the country, and some of the lackings that two main personality types in it are likely to feel. After that there's a light essay comparing Mozart and Bruce Springsteen. The section finishes with a look at the mind of the American businessman, showing how certain fears and religiously based notions explain national respect for the free market, and for working together.

Part Three is the single behemoth on money, mentioned earlier. In a big historical sweep, concentrating on money all the way, it tries to look even more thoroughly at the underpinnings of our attitudes.

The book ends with a Part Four about our ultimate goals, and the consolations we end up demanding against the fact that all these goals will be limited in some way by our own mortality. It is a problem seen in miniature in England's difficulties with creating an entrepreneurial culture like America's.

There was no way I could have done the research for all this without the excellent resources of the London Library in St James's Square. There I was able to enjoy all the personal attention of my little French village but with surprisingly little of the nosiness. The British Museum Library, and to some extent the Science Museum's historical holdings, filled in the bits the London Library lacked. The Pasteur archives in Paris were comprehensive on the great biologist. Going back further, William McNeill of the University of Chicago was probably responsible for first showing me how one could take long historical sweeps without falling into vague thinking; Leonard Olsen was important in introducing me to Aristotle as a living tool.

Tim Radford offered the ideas that first started me out on the Pasteur essay, and also helped in the overall editing; Matthew Hoffman, by disagreeing strenuously and sometimes even with reason with most of the ideas I have suggested to him in the past few years, has helped to clarify my thinking throughout. And Kathleen again managed, amazingly, to put up with it all.

Prologue

Prologue

Web of Words

Why do English people get constipated? Because they queue for the bus, they wash their face with flannels, they enter their houses on the ground floor, and they eradicate pencil markings with rubbers; that's why.

For Americans, everything is different. The equivalent American ailment, the one of maximum personal worry and occasional intimate revelation, is concern about the heart. And of course Americans do everything else differently. They line up for buses, wash with washcloths, enter their homes by the first floor, and never, ever eradicate pencil marks with a rubber: they erase them with erasers.

The difference is not one of fact, of course, but just in the words that members of the two societies use. Yet these words regularly line up on opposite sides of a great divide, and the attitudes controlling each side will give us some hint of the different feelings about sensation, power, anxiety and nature that different humans are prone to fall into.

The key difference in the British-American case is the separation out of the individual. Take the simple statement, 'the football team is planning to go to New York.' For a British person this would be glaringly ungrammatical. The correct form would be: 'the football team *are* planning to go to New York.' The American 'is' pulls the individuals into the group. Their uniqueness is lost. What counts, what is referred to, is only the unitary team. The British 'are' keeps the idea of the individuals as separate beings. The team may be planning to go somewhere, but that's only because each constituent member of it is agreeing to go.

This fits in with a different notion of sensation. As an American in Chicago I washed in the morning with a washcloth – a device whose name describes what it does: it's a cloth that washes. As an American in Britain I have to perform the same morning ablutions with a 'flannel' – a device that looks the same, but is wholly different in its linguistic psychology. The name of this object reassures me of how this object feels and what its content is – to wit, flannel.

The soothing confirmation of touch crops up in school. British schoolchildren use a rubber to scrape away their unwanted pencil marks. American schoolchildren have an eraser. 'Rubber' describes

7

the dual sensation of holding this cool, non-rigid substance and rubbing away with it. 'Eraser' says nothing about how it feels but just states the result: the mark has been erased.

Even for items that you can't feel, the British language will try to bring individual sensation into account. Consider that often helical metal or plastic device which is popularly used as a female contraceptive. If it's properly inserted, there's no way of feeling it once it's inside. The uterus doesn't have the necessary ascending sensory nerves. The closest substitute to direct touch you could get would be to look at it.

In Britain, that second-best attempt to get tactile knowledge is encouraged. The device is given the trade name of 'coil'; a name that describes how it looks, and corresponds with the real visual image a woman will have when shown a sample in her gynaecologist's office. In America the same device is universally called an IUD – short for intra-uterine device. The American name has nothing to do with anything the woman would actually see or touch. It's just an impersonal re-statement of the object's geographical siting.

In British English, such individual awareness is all. When Londoners queue for a bus, each one is making an individual choice: to queue. But when New Yorkers assemble for a bus, they are said to form a line. A line is a geometrical construct that might be visible from a helicopter flying overhead, but is by no means dependent on the wishes of the individuals who compose it. There is a lack of individual volition about a 'line'. A cluster of soldiers bullied by their sergeant into forming a column on a parade ground might be described as forming a line. No one would say that they formed a queue.

British motorists have a chance to respond individually, too. In switching from a motorway outside London to another road you enter upon a roundabout. The name aptly describes the disorienting sensation, the mass of swirls, curves and turns that you get driving around one of those concrete objects. But in America a 'roundabout' is unheard of. Drivers call the equivalent structure a clover-leaf, or a clover-leaf junction. This describes how a highway designer would look at it. On the drawing board or in aerial photographs it does look somewhat like a leaf of clover. But the American term gives no feeling of what it is like for an individual to scoot along one.

The same goes for 'elevator', as opposed to 'lift'. The American 'elevator' sounds like something performing an impersonal ascension. The British equivalent describes a piece of machinery which gives you the feeling of undergoing a lift when you're in it. The fact that only the British term describes a sensation is confirmed by usage in a different area. If an American child were playfully grasped and raised up by his father, he would never say that he had been 'elevated'. He would say, rightly, that he had been 'lifted'.

The terminology of train or jet travel follows the same rules. What counts to the individual traveller buying his ticket is the feeling that ultimately he will 'return', and that of course is the British ticket's name. In America you can only book that sort of journey by asking for a 'round-trip' ticket. This is an impersonal specification of a trajectory that could be charted on a map as a process of first going in one direction, and then in the other. There is no personal input into the exercise.

In all these cases, American English accepts that the individual will quite happily move about without caring how much attention the world immediately outside is giving him. In British English, that's impossible.

To get to an explanation it's useful to consider the utterance that's inescapable in large parts of the United States whenever you conclude a purchase or casual meeting: the exhortation to 'have a good day'. There is an awesome notion of an austere power somewhere that looks down and makes our days either good or bad. The stock phrase shows a belief in an organisation of human affairs where individual volition has no chance at all. Even the British formal equivalent – 'goodbye' – has a more individual sound: *I* am *personally* bidding farewell. The informal 'cheers' is even more clearly individualistic.

Why is all this? Are Americans colder, more impersonal, and concerned only with externals? Somehow that doesn't seem right for a country that produces jazz and rock music and the anything but impersonal paraphernalia of the Me Generation. What then?

I suspect it is because in America there's a feeling that the country was made by choice; it didn't just grow. If it grows, you are part of it and it will have been paying attention to you all the way along. But the state of being American is a matter of *joining* – of accepting a choice that someone else made.

Americans also will be conscious of living in a continent recently built up from scratch. That makes you used to thinking about the internal 'struts' of the world around you, and not so worried about how the end-products of those struts *feel*. The typical American city layout – that endless repetition of two-dimensional rectangular grids – both encourages and epitomises this impersonal thinking, the feeling of living within an X-ray.

A look at a few special fields might make all this clearer:

Nature. Walk though the front door of a British home and you emerge on the ground floor. To get to the first floor – the first one thought of as artificially constructed and imposed – you have to go one flight up. In America, the idea of the ground and all such instrusions of nature are banned from the house. Walk into a Texan's or any other home and you will be informed that already you're on the first floor. The host is reaffirming that he is no mere servant of nature, but its controller. The proud displays of plastic-wrapped vegetables in American stores, locking what once grew in dirt into safe plastic cells, make the same point.

Manners. Here it's curious that each country's best manners are quite neatly the other country's worst ones. An average American who doesn't know what to do at a party is likely to speak in a firm voice, and ask what profession the person he meets is in. This is violently unpleasant if it's a British person he meets. Similarly, the reserve and clipped phrases that a shy British person is likely to display at a party would be considered intolerably insulting behaviour by Americans he might meet there.

Now it is understandable that different national manners might offend. But it must be more than chance for them to offend so precisely. Our linguistic delvings show why. Americans at a party can do almost anything: to them the social system is given, and seems to exist independently. The British, however, must continually, by their actions and social references, re-create the social system they live in.

It's an exhausting obligation continually to have to prop up the world so. That's why British people are in constant terror of outstepping their place, doing something wrong, or just giving the wrong appearance. That would bring the whole precarious social world tumbling down. That's also why the postures and expressions of American tourists standing on the streets in London are so irritating to natives. The Americans are not terrified of outstepping their place. That ease, that independence from self and the self's willed position, undercuts the British approach to life and so is felt as an insult.

Tools. These provide a useful check on the argument that Americans generally speak as if the world is pre-set. A tool is, by definition, in the business of changing the external world. It is the one point where you can choose to break into and change your surrounding. This should reverse everything, making American usage subjective and British usage more objective. It is a simple matter of contrapositional logic, and I think the evidence backs it.

When an American wants to shift gears in his sports car he can put his hand on the gear shift. But a British driver has no such device immediately expressive of his will or intention there: he has to manipulate his vehicle through a gear 'lever'. More directly, when a person takes a certain tooled metal object in his hand to fit around and loose an obstinate bolt, he is likely to have to give it a wrenching burst of effort to get it to work. This felt sensation is incorporated in the American word for the device. It's called a wrench. The British term 'spanner', however, is only an arbitrary noun, or at best one that hints at the external specification of spanning a gap. This is a complete switchover from lines, erasers and clover-leafs, where Americans came out the cold, impersonally descriptives ones.

Similarly, electrical circuits in Britain reach the surface of a house's wall at an impersonal 'point' – just what a wiring diagram might label them as. In the United States, the place where an electric line surfaces in a wall is called a 'plug'. That's a term which describes perfectly what the ordinary person experiences whenever he uses it. His sole interest is the putting of a plug in there. Here, building up his world, getting involved with the internal struts, his surroundings do speak kindly and personally.

Body. Here's where we came in. The prime medical topic in Britain for commiseration among family members and close friends, perhaps, is constipation. In America a similar volubility and commiseration is more likely to be granted to imagined ailments of the heart.

Speaking a bit whimsically, if anything is discrete, individual, and empirical, it is constipation. Something appears, or it doesn't. The heart, by contrast, would be ideal as the American popular ailment. Hearts are things which have a central organising and controlling role. They are the perfect bodily metaphor for analogous events in the realms of American urban geography, society or language.

Conclusion? Language is a guide to the rules, the reminders, the idea machines encouraging us to stay in the world of the particular society we're landed in. It gives some hint of the great unexplored world of social presuppositions around us. But it also is a crude tool, a microscope that somehow you can never get into sharp focus. With language alone there will always be counter-examples, and important questions left hanging. How does a society 'know' to do all this? Can patterns this general explain our detailed politics today? Just what does it feel like for us to live inside these and other idea machines? For that we need to start again.

Part One
Two Themes

1

Socialism, Bacteria, and the Obsessions of Pasteur

I. AN IDEA

It was dinner time in the Pasteur house, and Louis was at it again. With his wife, daughters and sole son sitting in mortified silence around the table; with the usual dinner guest, Monsieur Loir, at the table with them; with the best tablecloth laid, the right plates out, the first course on, and the long-suffering maids in position at the side; with everyone set to begin the meal, the Professor began his hunt.

'He minutely inspected the bread that was served to him', Monsieur Loir wrote much later, in old age, 'and placed on the tablecloth everything he found in it: small fragments of wool, of cockroaches, of flour worms . . . I tried to find in my own piece of bread from the same loaf the objects found by Pasteur, but could not discover anything. All the others ate the same bread without finding anything in it.'

Then Pasteur went to work on the glasses. He lifted them up, peered at them closely, and wiped down each one he was going to use, hoping to remove all the contaminating dirt, which again no one else could see. He kept his fingers clean for the wiping, by refusing to shake hands with strangers or even friends during the day. The family waited, the maids and guest waited too, for all were used to the great man's obsession. 'This search took place at almost every meal', Loir continued, 'and is perhaps the most extraordinary memory that I have of Pasteur.'

What ever was going on? Had Pasteur gone bonkers, nuts, off his rocker? At first it's tempting to think so. If Mme Pasteur came home from the Galeries Lafayette and started tearing apart the family's food in search of non-existent wool and cockroaches, so that when her children returned they found her on the floor, legs out, hat askew and surrounded by great mounds of food in the kitchen, we could imagine that they would consider seeking professional help. But when it was their father who embarrassed them with his hunt

15

through the food they took it as normal. To some extent this was because he was the greatest scientist in France, and so had the prerogatives of the gifted. But I suspect even more important was that this pre-dinner hunting ritual matched almost exactly what Pasteur talked about when it was over and he finally looked up.

There are many accounts surviving of what personal conversation with Pasteur was like. In his loud voice, and with his sombre expression (there is only one known drawing, photo, engraving, or sculpture of Pasteur smiling), Pasteur would continually harp on two themes. The first of course was his laboratory work. During dinner at home he would recount with great satisfaction details of the mice he had eviscerated that day, or the purées of vaccinated spinal cord he had prepared, or whatever else he had done in his continuing, remorseless battle against the bacteria. Those bacteria were tiny infecting creatures that most people couldn't see, but which were always there, ready to pounce, to enter us and take over and grow. The hunt inside the dinner bread was no aberration with them around.

After the account of the day's laboratory work had run dry, Pasteur's monotone would turn to his second topic: politics. It was the only interest he held as strongly as bacteria. Some of his views were shared with all Frenchmen of his time, such as his great hatred of Germany, especially after the invasion of 1870–1. It was so strong that he devoted months of free work to the perfecting of French beer, so loyal patriots wouldn't have to drink that Boche muck again. Yet his main political view was not quite so universally shared. Pasteur was an extreme reactionary in politics. He ran (unsuccessfully) for the Senate on an extreme right-wing ticket, and in his letters recorded that the social high point of his life was a one-week visit with Louis Napoleon, at the Emperor's Palace in Compiègne.

The reason was simple. Pasteur had a horror of democracy. There was ordered society, which was good, especially if led by a strong man, and there was also a curious anti-society, a disordered thing of raw uncultivated bodies: the mob. That was a collection of small infecting creatures that decent people didn't ordinarily see, but which was always there, ready to pounce, to enter our society and take over and grow. It was what Pasteur and most right-wing Frenchmen thought had created the French Revolution, surging into existence on the streets of Paris; it was what had produced the Terror against the aristocracy, and the uprisings of 1830, 1848, and then – what Pasteur called a *saturnale* – the brief workers' takeover of the Commune in 1871.

Would someone coming late to the table know which of his two enemies Pasteur was going on about? The language of Pasteur and conservatives generally against the masses of the people was almost exactly like the language Pasteur had developed to use against bacteria. Both were everywhere, small swarming things ready to strike, to grow and propagate. They would destroy us in doing so, subvert our inner structure, have us collapse in disorder, and turn us into – the worst of all possible fates – a thing no different from the seething mass that had attacked. Let the mob take Paris and without the King or Emperor to shore us up we would dissolve into aimless bodies no different from the mob; let the bacterial mob take our physical body and we would decay into a putrefying bacterial mass no different from the attackers here either. If unpleasant entitites such as the people or bacteria had to exist, then they must be kept firmly in their place. The people, and especially the workers, were safe only if kept in passive Catholic trade unions, or state-run clubs, or other trustworthy bureaucratic bounds. The bacteria, in all their unpleasant and quick-to-grow varieties, were safe only if restricted to one slot in the Great Chain of Being, that of the decomposer of dead bodies, destroying order only after all life in it had naturally gone, and returning its atoms to the soil for rebirth. Outside of that, though, and they were terrible.

Which came first? There is some evidence that for Pasteur it was fear of the mob. His ideas about bacteria appeared pretty much fully formed in his first writings (1857) on the process of fermentation. In trying to explain how grapes turned into wine, and similar processes, he predicted the existence of living microbes, all apparently identical, yet autonomous, and which competed among each other in an attempt to grow on their target medium until they had fully taken it over. It turned out to be a good guess, but when he made it there was little evidence to back this or indeed any other detailed idea. Pasteur's other descriptions of bacteria, again generally before there was clear evidence to demonstrate it, also matched the view that extreme conservatives took of society. One was that the infection had to be stopped early (think of putting people who even might be revolutionaries in prison); another was that apparently weak individual organisms could cause the demise of large, complex bodies, i.e., that outside bugs could cause inside infection.

To us such views are standard, but at the time medical tradition thought otherwise. We have to imagine the scientific world before the germ theory of disease. When bacteria were found in wounds or sick people it was really thought of as an unimportant by-product of the true disease, which came somehow mysteriously from within and had to run its course. This is why doctors were so upset when Pasteur and others suggested that by not washing their hands between touching diseased corpses and touching healthy or somewhat healthy patients, they might be spreading disease. To the doctors this was preposterous. How could minute organisms cause disease in creatures so much larger? All authorities brought up in the old tradition concurred. Queen Victoria's medical advisors saw no need to clean up the no doubt typhoid-full cesspools near the water sources at Balmoral, from which she and the unfortunate Albert were encouraged to drink. Even Florence Nightingale never believed in 'infection', and was always against what in later life she called the 'germ-fetish'.

It was mere common sense – but for Pasteur it was a common sense which he saw, he *felt*, must be mistaken. An investigator with the standard medical view in mind, let alone one with a brain swept clean of all pre-hypotheses, could never have developed the whole concept of infecting microbes from the small evidence with which Pasteur began. But someone disposed to push forth this idea of small swarming things always ready to destroy order and take over; someone primed to find it anywhere he looked: he would be the one more likely to come up with the germ theory of disease.

Such similarities between social and scientific views have long been common – what better place to get fresh ideas than to just look around you? – and were especially so in the nineteenth century, when so many fields were being set up for the first time. When German professors discovered the approach of several million sperm to the human egg, which only one successfully penetrated, they described it as following the morally sound marriage patterns of the time. On one side there was a passive, waiting egg; on the other a crowd of rushing, eager sperm suitors, of which only the luckiest and strongest one would make it all the way into her affection – just as the professors might hope would happen to their own no doubt properly brought-up daughters.

From the pure evidence they had to work with this is almost all unjustified interpolation. The microscopes of the time could barely get any detail on the egg and its fine movements, and only produced a series of isolated, blurry images. From those static images one could just as well imagine the female with her egg being not passive but taking a more Boadicean approach to her men. This indeed is the standard view today: video microscope images and better *in vivo* techniques show that the sperm don't head towards the egg, but rush around randomly in all directions; it's the woman's body that directs them in, sometimes helped by an actively slurping cervix. Once drawn closer the sperm are dragged over the final approach by chemical trails the egg sprays out to energize and pull in a particular one. But this for the proper professors, if not their eager-to-boogie daughters, is not what they would have liked to see.

Maxwell's development of the kinetic theory of gases also seems to have come from his sharing in a standard view of society at the time. It was hard to tell what each individual in the great nation of England under Victoria was going to do, but somehow you could be sure that the end result of all those millions fussing, scurrying, slipping and interacting would be to man the navy, rule over the colonies, maintain a large coal industry, and do all those other things England was known for. This strangely cohesive power of the multitude, even though you could never tell what all the individuals in it were doing, was being described in detail by the new science of Social Statistics, and it was by explicit acknowledgement to it that Maxwell worked out his theory of gases where the scurrying molecules also were described only by overall statistics, and not individual biographies.

This sort of explanation sounds good, but it could become too deterministic. Should not every French conservative of the time who was aware of the problems of fermentation and disease have struck his head and said, 'Quelle bêtise! Of course the problem must be due to multitudes of blindly swarming bacteria! What else would make sense of my political phenomenology and analogical thinking?' In the Hollywood version, some of the big words judiciously dropped, that's no doubt how it would be. But as we know, such mass discovery did not occur: most French brows remained unslapped. Why Pasteur happened to be especially sensitive to this aspect of political society and worked it into his answers to the problem of disease, is a matter for the psychologist or biographer to answer. Our question now rather is: why did so many people at the time – so many of our own great-grandparents – go along with him? For the bacterial concept was not one of those scientific ideas, such as quantum mechanics, which ordinary people have a difficult time taking up. Rather it was like momentum, or computers: quickly accepted by all.

The first thing to note in an explanation is that, for humans, thinking by analogy is almost inescapable. Everything that works at one level we're keen to try to see in another one. I remember as a kid, when first learning about the solar system model of the atom, immediately wondering if our solar system was an atom in a larger being. Perhaps the gentle reader remembers the same.

Even easier is to compare what we see with our actual physical body. That, after all, is what we have to spend our lives immersed in. Children who draw the windows of houses to look like eyes so that the whole family home becomes like a larger body are doing just this. It is a very old technique, and was given wide spread in our culture through the notion of the Body of Christ. For long centuries that body was not just an analogy to society, but in the *corpus mysticum* was actually identified with the whole body of Christian society.

When we do compare the world to a body, we end up having to take into account that our own physical body is limited, both in prowess and, especially, in the fact that it will in time come to an end. Religion provides one consolation for this, but whenever men have strayed from religion there has been a need to find another consolation. Frequently this has meant finding something in the outside world to identify with that would provide that missing but so desired escape from mortality. In the late sixteenth century, legal and administrative documents began to note that the king had a natural body, which was certain to decay, but that the political body he was identified with was oh so very much better than that material one. Even in that early period those identifications with the Body Politic seem to be phrased wistfully, as if realizing it was only a second best.

In Pasteur's era the problem was becoming especially severe. Life was increasingly under rational control, so each loss of life seemed more objectionable, wrong. There also seems to have been a decrease in genuine popular belief in religion. The conjunction meant that there was an especially strong interest in altered forms of the body that had any sort of immortality to offer. One of these was patriotism, a continuation of that Kingly identification with the whole mass of living creatures in a political unit. But another, not a consolation but still a terrible fascination, was that mass of small creatures, that whole distorted society in miniature, which yet also happened to be immortal: the bacteria. Organisms known to science before that – cows, humans, daffodils – were not immortal. These were. The first journalists and royalty who peered through the microscopes in Pasteur's or Koch's laboratory to see the bacteria consistently reported this fascination.

Along with these factors of individual psychology, there were changes in the whole society to make Pasteur's concept so readily picked up in this particular era. The increased life expectancy meant that population was growing, a lot. Also there was a great amount of internal migration, from one country to another, and from the land to the city. There were perhaps 100 million more people in Europe in 1900 than in 1870. Strange things happened. In 1830 a swampy settlement by one of the American Great Lakes had a population of under 100. By 1890 it was the city of Chicago, with a population of one million.

There were not enough accepted institutions to handle all these new bodies. Guilds were gone, upper and middle society seemed closed, and so enormous numbers were left in between: working, or joining trade unions, or just being – always in those great numbers, always milling and jumbling and getting in the way of the established citizens and of each other. One would not need to have been M. Pasteur to be attuned to swarming masses with that going on.

Pasteur's idea doesn't explain everything about what came next. But since it encapsulated the basic critique of industrializing society, and since it did so in a form – those immortal little bacteria – that everyone could understand and which also had the oomph of scientific truth behind them: for those reasons it's worth tracing out what contribution to the modern era it did make.

II. CONSEQUENCES

In the late nineteenth century there was great public interest throughout the Western world in imperial questions, and perhaps never more so than late in 1898, when Kitchener's army descended from Cairo to do battle with the forces of the dervishes under the mysterious Khalifi, the successor of that Mahdi who had been responsible for the death of Gordon at Khartoum. Trailing along behind Kitchener were lots of new-fangled Maxim guns, and trailing along behind the Maxims, on foot, or pony, or commandeered camel, forming their own little group and distinguishable by their Oxford songs and swagger sticks and monocles and puttees, there were those most intrepid of creatures: the English war correspondents. There was Frank (the brother of Cecil) Rhodes representing *The Times*; Cross, who had rowed so magnificently with the Oxford Eight, for the *Guardian*; Bennett, another Oxford man, here on special assignment for the *Westminster Gazette*; and, above all, there was Steevens, probably the best writer of them all, who had an audience of over one million in Harmsworth's new *Daily Mail*.

What did these men report when Kitchener's army finally met the dervishes? Whatever they did must have touched a receptive spot at home, because newspaper circulations increased tremendously as the battle neared, popular excitement reached a level high enough to dishearten the few anti-imperialists left, and the collected dispatches these reporters produced as books in the few weeks immediately after the battle had extraordinary success, Steevens's alone going into thirteen printings in just a few months.

Their reports of the final battle, at Omdurman outside Khartoum, began with an attitude accepting extermination:

> **It was a fine day and we had come out to kill something.**
>
> (Bennett, *The Downfall of the Dervishes*, 1898, p. 161)

For what comes next there are two technical points to keep in mind. The British forces often formed their defensive lines amidst the local thorny shrub called the zeriba. And in their ranks there were large numbers of native recruits, often ex-dervishes.

Now the reporters were very aware of bacteria. Earlier the same Bennett had written about preparing water:

> **There can be no absolute guarantee against the intrusion of an evil bacillus into one's system. The only hope is that one's internal zeriba, so to speak, is well guarded by a valiant line of those good bacilli whose chief delight – so bacteriologists tell us – is to gather round the malignant invader and do him to death.**
>
> (Bennett, p. 133)

This is what the reporters ended up describing the enemy as: Kitchener's forces were taking the field against a huge number of bacteria! It began with a swarm:

> **The moment [officer Broadwood] saw them they began swarming up the hill.**
>
> (Steevens, *With Kitchener to Khartoum*, 1898, p. 271)

and it was a swarm that didn't properly die:

> **The officer . . . put a man-stopping revolver bullet in him but it didn't stop him . . .**

No white troops could have faced that torrent of death for five minutes, but the . . . blacks came on. [Their] lines gathered up again, again, and yet again: they went down, and yet others rushed on . . .

[Many] were torn to pieces, vermilion blood already drying on brown skin . . . [but] others again, seemingly as dead as these, sprang up as we approached, and rushed savagely.

(Steevens, pp. 285, 264, 269)

The difference from bacteria was that, while drugs against bacteria were only slowly being developed in laboratories, here in the laboratory of the Third World more developed techniques were available to do to the native what it would be really quite good to do to literal bacteria:

They came very fast, and they came very straight; and then presently they came no farther.

(Steevens, p. 263)

The Maxims and rifles rained bullets upon them . . . and they simply vanished from sight.

(Bennett, p. 172)

The battle was a success. Over 11,000 dervishes died against British losses of two officers and 23 non-commissioned officers and men killed. Omdurman and Khartoum were taken.

Now what is interesting is that what happened in the colonies was hardly ever like this. Native rebels were often well armed, or not swarming, or, as was the case almost everywhere Western forces went, there were no rebel forces at all to see. Yet somehow the British, American and French home populations and leaders were keen to pick out this particular, atypical event. Where the colonial war involved a lot of messy torture, murder of civilians, and small ambushes – as with the long US action in the Philippines – the home press didn't bother to pay attention. It's as if the interest was in the bacteria idea being displayed outward on to the colonies and the natives there. Could the people at home have been so simple as to do that?

The answer, I fear, is yes. The bacterial idea matched the basic nature of the growing society back home; it matched the deeper worries about bodily decay, and with our habit of merging levels it would be easy to superimpose those attitudes on to the much larger world of the colonies, which after all were bulging open the Great Power-controlled world system, just as the newly growing and migrating workers were bursting open the traditional order system at home. Plus, while no one wants to admit that they are thinking with another man's metaphors, there was no question that bacteria actually did exist. You just look under a microscope and there they are.

Since the bacterial idea was being so evidently proven true with the dervishes and other hordes that correspondents could scout out in the colonies, it got an added boost when applied back at home. There is a sense of urgency, of harshness, about social problems in this apparently tranquil period. Police chiefs and business leaders seemed to get a special glee in their planning sessions about how the Maxim guns could be turned on the city masses when needed; less blood-thirsty figures spoke out, with real concern, almost pleadingly, against unions and industrial strikes for better wages, not just on the grounds that companies couldn't afford it, but because – as we saw could happen with these dervishes! as might happen on Broadway or the Strand! – it would be the start of a full breakdown, disorder, social death.

The idea was so compelling that there was no reason to stop on the big level of the whole society. Dervishes and workers are but creatures outside us. Could the bacteria model reveal anything inside us? To match the bacterial properties that something would have to be primitive, and ready to swarm out at any minute, and also somehow strangely free from death. Well, we know what this describes: it is The Beast In Man. In this period people began to act as if they believed in, not just an abstract tendency towards evil or devilry in humans, that had been common enough in the past, but an actual, living beast, a creature which went extinct in the outside world but here lives on. The existence of germ plasm, which looked a bit like bacteria but which embryologists were showing was what grew to create human beings, revealed a way for this beast to exist.

There were lots of kooky variants. There was recapitulation theory, which seriously held that developing human embryos pass through all the evolutionary stages. There were anthropologists solemnly measuring criminals and workers to see how much of the beast's presence was revealed in their appearance. There was a new 'scientific' racism, which, with the help of popularized Darwinism, noticed the beast evident to an even greater extent in African or Asian peoples.

There were also two works of literature which reached extraordinary success on first publication, and with main characters whose names we still immediately recognize. The first was 'Dracula', and the second, my favorite:

It was a fine, clear January day . . . I sat in the sun on a bench . . . After all, I reflected, I was like my neighbours; and then . . . at the very moment of that vainglorious thought, a qualm came over me, a horrid nausea and the most deadly shuddering . . . I looked down; my clothes hung formlessly on my shrunken limbs; the hand that lay on my knee was corded and hairy. I was once more Edward Hyde.

was Stevenson's *The Strange Case of Dr Jekyll and Mr Hyde*.

Unlike traditional gothic, where characters would just be taken over by feelings of badness, this was the real stuff. We can tick off the parts of the bacterial essence in it. There is no way to resist the transformation, this takeover by the bad, destroying thing, when it comes out; it strikes directly at individuals; and, most distinctively, the bursting-out thing is an ancient remnant ('corded and hairy') which should by all rights have been dead long ago.

Before national statistics such as GNP, or workable macroeconomic theory, social changes were magic, strange, just popping out on us from who knows where. It was like dervishes appearing out of the desert; it was like looking down on your sensibly manicured and clean hands and seeing them begin to sprout hairs and claws. And if we didn't know exactly what to do at home, we did know that it was best to kill the dervish or any other foreign hordes; to fling down Stevenson's book at the end and be ready to kill any sub-human throwback who actually did exist.

With the First World War in 1914 that attitude began to be applied within Europe. Instead of the enemy expanding for dynastic ambition or other traditional reasons, he was now regularly treated as, quite literally, a mass of bacteria. Sections of the English press began to call the Germans 'GermHuns'. Vituperation within Germany was of a similar level. All this produced a terrible ferocity. Even a liberal paper such as the *New Statesman* wrote:

One desires the utter destruction of this evil thing [Prussianism] with as little scruple as one desires the end of an epidemic of scarlet fever.

(November 5, 1914)

Against a bacterial enemy that is the only action you can take.

For modern wars this was a new thing. During the Napoleonic wars Jane Austen in England had been able to go on writing her novels without having her plots or even her characters' conversation be bothered by the fact of the nation being at war. The regiment which marched into *Pride and Prejudice* (1813) is used just to dilly-dally with the ladies. Patriotism did not have to be hatred. In 1807, in the middle of the war, Humphry Davy, the leading and quite patriotic English scientist, saw nothing wrong with taking the boat and carriage to Paris to receive the Napoleon Prize from the French Institute for his work on electrolytes.

The last time in fact there had been the desire for extermination of the enemy within Western Europe was back in the Wars of Religion. That made sense then because God's ideas were held to be very true, and someone who had been taken over by the wrong one would certainly be incapable of correcting himself. He couldn't even be allowed to sit quietly at a distance from you, because he would have no choice but to try to act out his ideas against you. In the 1914–18 war it was not God but science, and especially biology, which was recognized as very, very true. And against an enemy who is responding to biology only death, again, can work.

With the Soviet Revolution in 1917, American and other Western troops were immediately sent into combat on Russian land to kill Soviets and try to crush the horrible new thing. There was much support for this back home, not just from the financiers who had investments to lose, but also from ordinary people. All societies, it was felt, were made of movable, potentially surging masses, only barely kept in order. Here they had burst out of that order. Ordinary people just had to imagine superimposing the yucky bacteria-ridden country on our own. It wasn't hard, as you could easily enough imagine superimposing a yucky and bacteria-ridden body on your own. The results would be terrible.

I sometimes wonder what would have happened if actual bacteria didn't exist on our planet, or hadn't been discovered. People would no doubt still have compared various levels with each other, that's basic, but maybe aspects other than that of potentially bursting-out swarms would have been what was picked out. There's no way to tell for sure. But in the world we are landed in bacteria did exist, and had been discovered; the matephor was promptly taken up. There was the description of Lenin being sent into Russia like a bacillus in his sealed train; the Quai d'Orsay's phrase *cordon sanitaire* to describe the policy of encircling that new entity over there across the steppes to keep its contamination from seeping out. Occasionally there were especially gifted politicians, such as the British Secretary of State for War and Air, who in just a single rolling sentence could make it seem not at all crazy that events at one level should jump magically through space and have an effect at another. Superimposing germs, bodies, countries, and thundering hordes, Churchill wrote:

Eastward . . . lay the huge mass of Russia . . . a poisoned Russia, an infected Russia, a plague-bearing Russia, a Russia of armed hordes smiting not only with bayonet and with cannon, but accompanied and preceded by the swarms of typhus bearing vermin which slay the bodies of men, and political doctrines which destroy the health and even the soul of nations.

(*Evening News*, July 28, 1920)

But this even Lloyd George found excessive.

In America the anti-Russian outrage was matched, as we might by now expect, with a search for dangerous, treacherous, body-politic-destroying creatures at home. The Attorney General organized a series of raids on private homes in 1919 to arrest and then deport what he called 'thousands of aliens . . . direct allies of Trotsky'. That almost all were quite patriotic Americans, and many were just elderly immigrants with the misfortune to have non-American-sounding names, didn't stop the glee, and the righteousness, with which the deportations were carried out. Those who carried the foreignness and hints of that submerged beast directly in their bodies would be even more directly bad; laws were passed to halt Eastern European and Mediterranean immigration.

After the Second World War the attitude towards foreign and especially poor countries continued to be that they were huge storehouses of potentially swarming hordes. If even a drop of the infection from Russia – where the swarm had already been unleashed! where the germ of disorder and dissolution was nourishing! – landed on them, they would of course be triggered to swarm out. In 1946 *Time* magazine showed a large map of the world, with each country on it in one of the three colors. Why? The map was labelled

COMMUNIST CONTAGION

and, as the legend explained, the colors showed whether the countries were 'safe', 'exposed', or already 'infected'.

Time also pointed out that Marxism calls for the spread of revolution around the world. There is a curious selectivity about such charges. Marxism also calls for everybody to be equal. But the people who ran Russia weren't equal with their subjects, as indeed Western powers pointed out. If that part of their professed teachings wasn't followed, what reason was there to think that the rest would be? You need to have preconceived ideas about your enemy to pick just one strand as unerringly as that.

The founders of the US policy of containment against the Soviet Union held strictly to the swarming disease view. In his *Foreign Affairs* article first proposing the policy, George Kennan wrote:

For we have seen that Soviet power is only a crust concealing an amorphorous mass of human beings.

The consequences of all this we know pretty well. The Truman White House looked at Greece and saw that, as Dean Acheson put it in a meeting with Congressional leaders:

The [Soviet] corruption of Greece would infect Iran and all to the east. It would also carry infection to Africa.
                                        (*Present at the Creation*, p. 219)

With that in mind it wouldn't matter that what Truman was actually asking for was guns and salaries for a most unpleasant group of recently pro-Nazi Greek royalists. Similar proxies were found elsewhere. Clearly they couldn't be communists, but it was also very important not to have reformist or humane anti-communist leaders in those countries. All those types were soft on workers or peasants. You start by being soft, you end up by losing control. Only with a hard man in power could we be sure we were safe, whence Rhee in Korea, those generals in Central America, our capable friend the Shah in Iran, etc. Since China was one of the worst sources of possible surging bodies – the Yellow Peril of many years' repetition – little countries on its border would have to be especially well supported.

Also, it would be the appropriate thing to bomb population centers. This had been talked about earlier, between the wars, as soon as airplane technology looked like making it possible. There was some sense in this. City centers are where a lot of important equipment and factories are likely to be. But the attitude seemed somehow more than that; it was as if by aiming at cities you would somehow be getting at the core of the beast. Early bombing expeditions by the British in the Middle East against native populations between the wars were calmly talked about with that attitude. After the war there was an almost total American acceptance of the rightness of targeting atomic bombs on Soviet cities. The ferocity of the recent war against Germany and Japan was probably necessary in getting citizens used to such means, but without the underlying swarming disease idea there would have been no reason to propose the end which required those means.

Joe McCarthy's speeches were a skilful description of what you get when you superimpose the bacterial and Soviet images at home again. The main point that he and his young friends such as Nixon and Bobby Kennedy pushed was that there were spies at home, huge numbers of them, all over the place, and that they were weakening us in battle against the main external evil. As he put it:

The Communists within our borders have been more responsible for the success of Communism abroad than Soviet Russia.

The spies are simply the contamination spreading through our national system. As we weaken, and become less like what we should be, we help it along. One consequence of accepting this attitude was the great conformism in America of that period. It was imperative that the normal, traditional, social bonds be maintained. A break-down of such bonds would have been a sign that the infection – the breakdown of the usual order arrangements – was underway.

Today the Pasteur idea is still going strong. It helps explain why conservatives are so against policies to help the poor at home: who wants to help the creature breed in our midst? It suggests how attention on crime can maintain a feeling against the Russians, for wouldn't a takeover by the Soviet Union or its ideas break our remaining barriers against internal disorder and release these savages in our midst? It is there murmuring distrust in the background when problems with strategic treaties with Russia arise, it keeps us viewing the Warsaw Pact as a horde just waiting to surge out, and, especially, it helps explain the curious response of Reagan and so many Americans to the revolution in Nicaragua.

To many European observers what happened there had merely seemed a case of a government of bad guys taken over by a

government of better, if admittedly not perfect, guys. But this is
wrong. It was spreading entities from the evil empire, not poverty or
local desires for reform or anything like that, that produced the
Sandinista goverment:

**It was a dark day for freedom when [the] Soviet Union
spent $500 million to impose communism in Nicaragua.**
(Reagan in the *Washington Post*, June 6, 1985)

If the public could be made to see the danger and zap the badness
everything would be all right. But since they were recalcitrant, weak
with memories of those body bags coming back from Vietnam, it
would for the time being just have to be isolated as you would any
infectious disease. Arms were sent to the surrounding countries, and
when an American battle fleet of nineteen ships and 5,000 troops was
sent to further hold back the bad thing down there, Reagan's aides
spoke of it (*New York Times*, July 23, 1983, p. 1) as

a possible quarantine

around Nicaragua. The President was insistent on the badness that
could spurt out from there:

**The Sandinistas [are] . . . creators of a fortress Nicaragua
that intends to export Communism beyond its borders.**
(Reagan's radio speech, February 17, 1985)

That is what would happen if the quarantine failed. Once again there
was the vision of swarming bodies: we were heading for a

tidal wave of refugees.
(Reagan in the *Washington Post*, June 21, 1983)

How exactly were these bodies to reach us? Sometimes the
administration was reasonable about this, as in Reagan's big May 9,
1984 speech where he described how a country could gradually build
hostile military bases closer and closer to our borders. But sometimes
he was rather more excitable, as when in March 1986 he declared,
imploring comprehension of the danger, that Nicaragua was

**a privileged sanctuary for terrorists and subversives just
two days' drive from Harlingen, Texas.**

Looked at literally this could be ridiculed:

The driving distance between Harlingen . . . and Managua, capital of Nicaragua, is 2,098 miles . . . Experienced truckers take three to four days . . .

'You've gotta have it floored the whole way and never stop to make it in two, I would think,' said David Allex, president of the Harlingen Chamber of Commerce.
(*Washington Post*, March 16, 1986)

But it wasn't meant to be taken literally. It was just a reminder of what sudden irruption here would be. Anyone ready to superimpose levels could understand that.

The real Nicaragua didn't matter. It was a small country, far away, of which we knew little. What counted was that the purported change there struck at home. That was what was so understandable, and worse than any physical invasion by Commie Latinos. That was why so many voters who had doubts about Reagan's tactics still agreed that we would be a lot better off without the Sandinistas. The change from Somoza to Sandinistas, the reversal of order, represented an attack at the key points of America today. Indeed it even hinted, horribly, at the precariousness of those points. Who would want that? It would be like bringing up prostates and sagging breasts at a society dinner. It would be like talking about the body's ultimate decay in death. It would, indeed, be as ill-mannered as bringing up bacteria at the dinner table.

Which is, after all, what the whole story is about.

2
Pasteur II: Hitler's Bacteria

It is illuminating, if distasteful, to examine why Hitler and his movement were so obsessed by the notion of the Jews as being, not just any disease, but specifically an example of the new-style bacterial disease. They went on about it at tremendous length, not just in official writing and speeches, but in informal talk over the dinner table, personal letters, etc:

> **The discovery of the Jewish virus is one of the greatest revolutions the world has seen. The struggle in which we are now engaged is similar to the one waged by Pasteur and Koch in the last century. How many diseases must owe their origins to the Jewish virus! Only when we have eliminated the Jews will we regain our health.**
> (Hitler, as recorded by a shorthand note-taker over dinner,
> February 22, 1942)

> **We have exterminated a bacterium because we do not want in the end to be infected by the bacterium and die of it. I will not see so much as a small area of sepsis appear here or gain a hold. Wherever it may form, we will cauterize it.**
> (Himmler to his officers)

The identification with microbes was comprehensive and insistent. Why?

To find out it's necessary to return to turn-of-the-century Vienna, fief of the Habsburgs; city of opera and slums, Christian Socialists and Social Democrats; city of workers and painters and prostitutes and dreamers; city where the impressionable young Hitler lived from 1907 . . .

Vienna was immensely larger than it had been half a generation before: in space, in population, in complexity of internal not-quite-worked-out arrangements. The established order of the Habsburgs,

33

which had once been like a tight fist holding the populace, was now a fist being splayed open by the gush of all the new creatures, pushing and clammering and forcing their way out of the hold.

At the heart of this change were of course the workers. There were more than before, they did not have established places to go to as before, and even when the instructions for their appropriate sequestering in the lower reaches of the industrial hierarchy were given, they did not do the decent thing and obey, follow orders, sit where pointed to, but instead they objected, fussed, and pushed and shoved out from where the prior system would have wanted them to go. They didn't fit, they didn't want to fit, and as a result everyone suffered: that awful scurrying growth spread and pushed open the hierarchial fist even more.

That was step one, and most people would have been content to end there: railing against the workers, the ingrates, the confusion. Not so a young man convinced that he had a special vision, a genius; that he could see deeper than others, into the essence of the world and its ideas. If the workers were in a discomforting in-between spot in Viennese society, threatening the whole, one would just have to face up to the problem of in-between spots. One would have to look, hard, where other men didn't dare. One would have to ask why.

It could not be because the workers chose to be so difficult about accepting a proper place. They were too stupid to choose. They were not special, gifted, capable of world-shaking gesture. It had to be because they were led. And there was no question who was leading them: it was the Social Democratic Party. Even that everyone admitted. But look harder and you could see what no one admitted: that Social Democratic Party was secretely being led by the Jews. One more step of transitive logic and you had it: the Jews were at the interstitial spots weakening and threatening all society!

When I recognized the Jew as the leader of the Social Democracy the scales dropped from my eyes. A long soul struggle had reached its conclusion.

(Mein Kampf)

This is the reasoning we have seen so many times before. The problem of the strange and unpleasant deformation of society is reduced to its essence. That essence is not left floating around in the realm of invisible ideas. An actual living individual or type of individual is found who accords to it. For Pasteur or at least those who looked to his work, that concrete summary, that catechismic shorthand, had been the bacteria. For others it was now to be the Jews.

It's fitting that a slightly aimless Austro-German should be so ready to notice this. Germany itself was the odd man out in the heavyweights of the European Great Power system. Everything it tried was not quite good enough: fit only to let it squirm into the little gaps left open by the oversight of the others. Their parliament was impressive, but not quite so distinguished as the great English or French parliaments; their efforts to get into the colonial system too were second-best, consigned to leftover spaces: a scrap of Southwest Africa here, an island nobody else cared to pick up there. Within that culture the artistic career of Hitler in Vienna from 1907 was more of the same: unsuccessful efforts to break in, to slip his drawings into the extra space at that exhibition; a failure made clear by those dreadful doss-houses he had to return to each night, unwashed, unsituated; not respectable middle class, yet not even solid working class with the associated community that might suggest. In fact Germany was at the forefront in industrial chemistry and electromagnetic theory and mathematical logic, but to get pride from that you had to get pride from science; and science, with its associated ideas of rationality, fairness and non-subjectivism, was not something that men in the young Hitler's position were inclined to appreciate.

His problem and that of many Germans was one where boundaries have been made clear, the main entities have been clearly defined, and yet you're not allowed to pass those boundaries, to slip into those entities. It's like looking at a field of great translucent bubbles, each with happy individuals or worlds inside them, but when you scamper up to the field the bubbles transmute and turn into solid boulders: hard, locked, impervious to any effort you make to try to break in; consigning the outsider to slipping between the spaces, clambering over and around and between but never within, never right in the centers where the real life, the real concentrations of meaning, are going on. This had been a problem even within Germany for a long time: their polity was a collection of separate entities, and even after unification under Bismarck it remained one that could, so easily, as the Great Power neighbors so clearly would like, be broken apart again into those mutually excluding blocs. This is perhaps the reason residents of that country were reported in so many visitor's letters and journals to be excited about dirt; to have an eye out for it; a concern for clearing and cleaning and generally keeping control of it; dirt being *par excellence* a substance that is not quite any one clear entity we know or can identify (were it so it would not be dirt), but a little bit of this, a little bit of that – a perfect representation of that which is between the rules, between the proper entities, perpetually slipping around the main blocs of life.

This concern will naturally lead to picking out the Jews. Stare at in-between spots in society, and even if you don't follow the reasoning that leads from workers to the SDP to their Jewish leaders, you will have reason to find the Jews there. Members of a religion opposing yet linked to the dominant one are at the weak and threatening points of society if anyone is. By their existence they put it in doubt. The priest says Christianity is totally true and the serfs agree it's totally true but these guys in their funny hats raise doubts. Prominent among the anti-semitic brochures available to Hitler in Vienna were translations from *Civilta Catholica*, the organ of the Jesuit order, where Jews were explained to be responsible for the French Revolution, for liberalism, for crucifying children, etc. Even if the Jews don't say anything, the mere fact of them being around suggests that the accepted relationships in society might not be true.

This is what all the old charges about the Jews poisoning the wells seems to be trying to say. Water is a pure and clearly defined central category, the definition of what is non-dirt if you will. It then becomes only a way of making clear what we think of the Jews to imagine them poisoning those water souces, switching them from pure to non-pure. The Jews are a concentrated form of interstitialness in society at all times, and never more so than in turn-of-the-century Europe, when they've been emancipated, allowed to drop the hats, and infiltrate even closer into the center of society.

That's why Hitler naturally associated the one concentrated essence, the Jews, with that other concentrated essence, the bacteria. Both occupied the same conceptual spot. Both were the weak link, the threatening binding strand: horribly within and yet not of us. And the reason they were both there, overlapping so suggestively, was not mere chance, a quirk, bemusing coincidence, but because both came from the same broad critique of a quickly industrializing society. One might even expect that the hastier that industrialization had been, the stronger these critiques would be, and so, roughly, it was.

In Eastern Europe, more quickly industrializing Slovakia was harsher on the Jews than the adjacent Subcarpathian Rus; more quickly industrializing Poland was worse than adjacent Lithuania. In

Western Europe from about the 1880s to 1914 the industrial and urban transformation of society was least extreme in Britain (where the main structural change had occurred already), about the same or a bit stronger in France, and without question greatest of all in Germany, which had started latest, and come on fastest. If you view it as a rising slope, from the flats around the Thames, then sliding up across France all the way to a peak in Germany, then the trend of entrenched anti-semitism would match it, with local bumps and falls, all the way along. There were other factors, but this was a big one. Should not cleanliness and disease mania be highest on the peak too?

There was even the scientific quirk that while bacteria had been uncovered back in the nineteenth century, and their discoverers lauded as saviors, for several decades after it was not possible to find a remedy against all of them. This increased the excitement. The problem was still there, all around, constantly discussed, like AIDS now or polio in the early 1950s, the cure imminent and more tantalizing because of that. There were even national divisions in the bacterial search. Germans took especial pride in the tuberculosis baccilus, since it was their own Koch who had the credit for revealing it. (France clung more to rabies *à la* Pasteur.) It's no surprise that Hitler's earliest letters and talks identify the Jews particularly with that popular tuberculosis baccilus.

And the consequences of this identification? Those we know only too well. In the light of the bacterial model, we can see how they were linked and made sense, and indeed could only have received the force needed for action by having such a conveniently summarized model, encapsulating the standard critique of modernity and its new social organizations. Even well before Hitler was in power, public hygiene measures with an ominous ring were getting started. Isaac Bashevis Singer describes, as a Chasidic boy in German-occupied Warsaw during the First World War, having his street being suddenly surrounded, armed German soldiers leading out all the Jews, women and children included, their being herded to special reception centers, their clothes being removed and replaced by simple gowns, and then being led in great confusion and with children crying to large 'spraying' rooms where they were . . . merely dusted with powder to remove the lice and bacteria that were on their bodies (typhus actually was a problem), and could otherwise lead to infection for the Germans in these freshly occupied lands.

Then, with Hitler and the Second World War, the final identification step was made. There was the invasion of the Soviet Union, to root out the Jewish infection sources there. There was the declaration of war on the United States just days after Pearl Harbor – an apparent mystery as the Wehrmacht had just been stopped outside Moscow, America looked content to go to war with Japan only (a move which had long terrified Churchill), and there was no treaty between Japan and Germany forcing support for Japan in these circumstances; but it was no mystery at all when one realizes the great stickiness of causality, the necessary interlinks of order and the right principles. If the assault on Russia had failed it was because of a basic bacteriological mistake; pure sources of Jewish infection had been left untouched, in the USA, and would now have to be battled with directly.

There was also, throughout, the hunt for the Jews wherever the German army gave the opportunity; the mobile field squads to purify on the spot; or the local police, the trains and death camps. The individuals so collected might not look dangerous – children, women, peasants, quiet rabbis – but that was just the thing: bacteria don't look like anything at all.

That's what is special, and eternally dangerous, about Pasteur's bacteria. They are invisible. The enemies, the sources of evil that they predicate, are ones which ordinary people cannot make out, however closely they peer or stare. You need specialists to find bacteria, men with microscopes and university training. You also need specialists to find conceptual taint, conceptual threat, and its possible sources of infection. It might be Stalin with his inquisitors, it might be Joe McCarthy with his committee lawyers; it might be Thatcher with her 'enemies within' or even nice, amiable Reagan, with his killing policy towards the Nicaraguans and other dangers; it certainly was Hitler, hunting to find every one of those human vermin, with his institutes of racial purity to decide even the slightest unclear case. Our century has supported them all. They will be gone when the problems of modernity are gone; when we are content with how things are going, and who's making the changes and where. But until that distant date let us leave them as a warning, on display, all together; let us leave them joined with the image of Pasteur at his dinner table, searching, searching, for subversion, the source of decay, which they know is there – and which everyone around will take their word for, even though they see not a thing.

The next essay looks into the old, old question of how we choose to act, to explain why there is such support for fearsome weapons systems these days – and also for one most curious sort of modern hero . . .

3
Commandos from the Invisible World

Lieutenant William Taylor, troop commander in the elite Delta Force commandos, veteran of combat in Korea and Vietnam; commended for night attacks in North Vietnam and Grenada; Lt. Taylor, his body honed to a fine pitch, Kevlar body-armor on under the weapon harness holding his HK machine-gun, grenades, and hand-gun; Lt. Taylor, finally, on special assignment with the British SAS, dangling on a rope outside the Iranian Embassy in London as his team's commando assault was under way, grabbed the arm of his colleague on the next rope, stared resolutely in his eyes, and then began to make a strange noise. It had something in it of a grunt, something of a high-pitched whine: there were two short 'aeh's and then a long 'bdduh-mmm-mmm-mppph!': Lt. Taylor was in tears.

'I'm sc-c-c-ared', he blubbered, his lower lip trembling, tears rolling from his eyes, 'I-I, I . . .' – he stopped, looked at the ground twenty long feet below, then in a strained, whimpering voice called out 'If I resign now you can't make me go!' The BBC cameras with telephoto lenses rolled on.

Wait. Stop. Try again. Lt. William Taylor, troop commander in the elite Delta Force commandos, decorated veteran etc.; Lt. Taylor, in the secluded Polynesian hut with the young native girl Larsi, watched as she slowly undid the simple knot in one shoulder of her dress strap. She undid the knot over the other shoulder, and let the thin cotton material fall to the bamboo floor. She stood proudly, legs apart, revealing her tanned, naked, and willing body. The air was still, and hot, and sweat beaded on her skin. She dropped the peel of the banana she had been slowly eating, and took a tentative step forward, the fine muscles on her hip tautening over delicate skin as she moved. The Lieutenant stepped forward too, his shirt half off already, his grizzled, masculine torso revealed.

The girl's eyes were limpid as he reached for the zip on his combat fatigue trousers, then dilated as he slipped on the peel on the floor, and had his feet shoot up as he crashed downwards, his hand on the zip continuing to pull it wildly in a reflex motion as he tumbled through the air, the result, as his trousers slipped lower in the contortions of his fall, a case of near, and quite unextractable, vivisection. The native girl gasped; then giggled, grabbed her dress, and left.

The images are preposterous ones, because we do not expect our military elite to bumble. They are to be cool, implacable: hardened to a mission and capable of carrying it out come what will. That's what is so attractive about them, what makes them so popular and esteemed. They are certainly not supposed to get queasy and blubber while abseiling down the wall of a terrorist-infested embassy; they are not supposed to bumble and do unmentionable things to their private parts in more intimate moments either.

The vision of cool, efficient killers is such a compelling one that during the Achille Lauro incident back in October 1985 (when a cruise ship was hijacked and the culprits later intercepted in the air) even a liberal paper like Britain's *Guardian* fell in with the standard image in the world press of seven American F-14 Tomcat fighters 'scrambling' from the deck of their aircraft carrier to intercept the Egyptian passenger jet carrying the four Palestinian hijackers. What does this image of hi-tech scrambling mean? A rush, at maximal efficiency, the finest harmony of man and machine possible, carrier hydraulics, jet ignition, pilot surmounting of g-force acceleration, then a flawless handling of high-powered engines. Once in the air the pilots streak direct to their target and assemble in perfect formation around it, not cocky but just assured that they're doing it right, that they're doing it perfectly. Simply 'taking off' would not have been enough. Having *scrambled* they are forced, pressed to the limit. There is no room for volition or possibly imperfect choice: chance is removed from their every act.

The story loses some of its impact, however, when several days later the *Washington Post* points out, on the evidence of servicemen on the carrier during the mission, that the F-14 pilots intercepted several other planes first before getting the right one. This suggests a whole different world. Here we see hillbillies, hicks, aerial bumblers. If they entered in assured formation around the first plane they streaked to, that was wrong: a formation that had to be dropped, with apologies, muttered excuses over the radio, while another possible passenger plane was picked out, the pilots trying to figure out in the dark if it was the right one this time, quibbling among themselves, one charging the others with bad navigation perhaps, maybe the second answering back defensively, the third going into a sulk, the fourth clearing his throat and tentatively questioning, drawling over the radio to the next plane they stumbled across, to ask just who the pilot was, ready to be humiliated again, to make embarrassed excuses again, to have to trundle through the Mediterranean night over to another vague mark on their radar.

Military operations are almost always like this, from mass battles to what are supposed to be precision commando raids, as retired veterans will most volubly explain. Even the lore of missiles, which is linked in the popular view with the implacability and perfection of the commando, turns out to not be quite what people think when you talk to servicemen who have had to work with them. Those shoulder-held SAM-7 missiles which were supposed to have devastated assaulting armor in the 1973 Middle East war were in fact fired thousands of times for only a few tens of confirmed kills. That is not very perfect. Similarly for the SAM-6 missiles used by the Egyptians against Israeli aircraft – which missed an estimated 98–99 per cent of the time in that war – or the much-publicized missile installations around Hanoi, which accounted for only about 8 per cent of the downed American bombers there, as compared to 85 per cent downed by guns (the remainder by MiGs).

Since people who have served in the army will most likely never have seen cool, efficient killers, human or electronic, on the loose, what about the rest of us? Here too there's a problem. Commando assaults, or implacable Mafia hit-men, are rarely seen in our neighborhoods. That leaves hardly anyone who has seen them in real life. Yet still the image persists:

Missilery is what people are all enthused about.
Thomas Hahn, staff member of the House Armed
Services Committe, in Connell, *New Maginot Line*, p. 50.

Still people respond, eagerly, to the notion of the man-machine, of implacable individuals or devices, set on a goal, organizing it perfectly, whom no thing, no one, can possibly deter. Why?

The answer, I suspect, begins precisely with this fact of cool killers being so rare in our ordinary lives. There is one kind of living, which we do, where people bumble, and stumble, and are never quite sure that what they're doing is right; and there is another, more attractive kind, the opposite extreme, where an action, once selected, is begun and carried out without pause.

In literary terms what we have is the difference between comedy and tragedy. Let what are the generally invisible requirements of necessity start acting clearly on us and we have tragedy, people being propelled around by that which is and must be. It's like stepping on a fast escalator. But let people try to step out of those pre-ordained roles – wave their arms and frantically try to race off the escalator they're caught on – and we have comedy. It's where Oedipus pulls on a Groucho Marx face-mask and says *What King? –* I never heard of the guy, you better go somewhere else to find him. The audience boos and walks out, saying it's not a tragedy. They're right.

Only the commandos are guaranteed a better ride. We, and they, begin by standing somewhere in a huge, three-dimensional scaffold-ing. But whereas we so disquietingly feel lost in this labyrinth of life's possibilities, an unclear haze around us not knowing which path forward to take, they are pulled irresistibly along the right route in it, just the echoing thud of their combat boots left behind to show us how easy it can be. Something is speaking to these men, showing them the true way forward. Something we are unable to directly see, however we strain our eyes. But, from the evidence of these commandos, so certain on their missions, something which we now know is there.

II.   THE OTHER SIDE

The concept is, of course, an ancient one. Plato, Jesus, Buddha and many others have insisted on there being two worlds – the first being the usual setting of daily life, and the second, the backdrop one where necessity and certitude of action are maintained, being generally hidden, yet immensely potent when it does happen to break through.

For a long time no one would have needed to be reminded of this, but in the west for quite a few generations now people have become used to spending much of their life in areas where the two once separate worlds seem to have finally merged. One of these is science, where the laws of God, the inner rules controlling how all nature and the universe works, are felt to be no longer existing up there in heaven or the Lord's mind, no longer such that you can only hope to figure them out by studying theology and the minutest phrasings of the Testaments, but rather are held to exist entirely down here, actually within the material objects they are supposed to rule. In the old view you could sing out Grace before a meal with real feeling, real belief that you were speaking to a higher power responsible for the food before you; with the new view we either skip Grace, or perhaps just mumble it, embarrassed: for the food now is a product of earth and fertilizers and other clearly non-spiritual, clearly non-holy, things entirely down here – not of God or anything else Up There.

The second of these now merged realms would have been even more extraordinary for our ancestors to behold: it is what we call economics. The idea that man can control his life, hew out by himself the income and position he will enjoy – for long centuries this was blasphemy. The rules which controlled all our doings, all our fate, were Up There, not something we mortals down here could hope to decipher. How could we? Miserable sinners, playthings of God's will, don't have that right. Only free economic agents, what the advancing economies of the past century or so have allowed so many of us to become, can do so.

Now what's interesting is that despite this apparent merging, despite our accepting of the scientific view that kicked God out of the upper heavens so that there was no real place for any Other World to exist, let alone communicate to us, a surprisingly large number of individuals have been unable to let it vanish. It's had to become different, you can't keep it loaded with God or angels, that's too unsubtle – but it's still there.

One of the most common of these holdovers is of a particular Other World existing behind us, an ectoplasmic hard to physically grab on to realm, which is stuffed full entirely with the magic that allows humans to become creative. Adults find it difficult to hook up to it, unless they happen to be geniuses; it is only children who have no problem in finding the portals – the feeding nozzles dangling from the sky – through which they can be fed the power that makes their paintings and songs and stories so original.

In Freud's view the background world is slightly different; one stuffed solid with rampant sex lust this time. It too can reach through to humans, but only at those most noble of possible moments: a successful session of therapy at the psychoanalyst's office. It might be 19 Berggasse, it might be in thick-carpeted offices in Hampstead or Manhattan, yet wherever the patient's reminiscences are properly guided, contact will be made, and out the dark, controlling world will gush. End the session, and the cork is popped back in; the world's store of suppression will not leak out uneconomically.

Western legal systems are much like Freud. There is a background, all-pervasive thing called justice. Usually it's off away from us, not visible in the messy and unordered world of daily life. Only in one place will it flash across the gap and make its appearance in our world: this favored spot is the courtroom. To help prise it out you will need judges, who, since they have the same role as the psychoanalyst, will lead the witnesses in a process of remembering. Once their words are positioned just right, out the 'justice' from the background world will emerge, gushing forth in the panelled courtroom.

These examples are secular, but the religious origins are still clear. Justice is speaking to us from what used to be thought of as heaven; the Unconscious and its demons from what used to be thought of as hell. The psychoanalyst is a priest, the patient is his ritual, and the revelations of childhood repression or trauma are statements from the otherwise hidden devils. Similarly for the enrobed courtroom justices, their ritual of the trial, and the emergence of a clear message from Beyond. It is all a convenient triad, because if the gods or devils are obtuse, the priest can change the rules. Psychoanalysts can decide on the spot what constitutes a patient's revelation, court judges can use different precedents to be sure of selecting an aspect of the trial that will produce a verdict, and priests can say Whaddya mean that smoke from the embers isn't a good sign. The priests/analysts/judges are not necessarily lying. They don't need to, because they believe the background thing is there.

There are probably several reasons for the whole rigmarole. The existence of a 'certainty realm' gets over our unease about what to choose. Also it has long been a good way for rulers to boss people around: the 'I personally don't need it but the gods insist that you give me half your crops' approach. (A compelling nation-state in the background has been a common, and much reinforced, replacement.) Our ready resort to thinking by analogy makes it even easier. The past is one big chunk of necessity we are all aware of – what happened is fixed for all time – so having other hunks of solidified necessity around is not that strange an idea. Imagine that necessity spreading not just over the past but through the present and into the future too, and there you are with a nice image of this Other Side. We can back up anything we want to do by reference to that. Admittedly there will be a blurring of the 'you shoulds' of daily argument with the 'you had tos' that cement up the past, but while logicians might object, most humans can put up with that.

Something like this is going on, I suspect, when religious believers feel they can best pull God through by coming together in places where their social necessity is at its strongest. A Martian observing a church or mosque or synagogue would see humans going to a place where they restrict each other with the greatest fervor – don't talk, sit like this, now talk and say precisely this, swing the ornament precisely that way, etc. It is a way of acting out the logical similarity of the backdrop second world – in this case God – to social necessity: our 'musts' are made so strong, the strongest we can, that there God's presence pops out in the process.

The examples are not just to debunk – I prefer a world with courts to one without; I admire the ethical good some religions can encourage – but to show the range of underlying imagery into which different thinkers, at different times, have put this notion of two difficulty-communicating realms. Indeed our linguistic convention of 'underlying reality' and 'underlying truth' is probably more of the same, with we in that case being the lucky oracles.

III. TWO TYPES OF OBLIGATION

For Delta Force, the SAS, and hi-tech weapons generally, the historical linkages of interest are the ones that have been worked out where theology touches on ethics. Here, the evidence being slight, the debates have accordingly been ferocious. In early Christian theology Pelagius, the Welsh ecclesiastic who lived in the late fourth century, made the mistake of suggesting that we live our lives almost entirely in this world, and accordingly make our moral choices freely, with no need for outside help, certainly not intervention over from the other side by God. For this he was damned in quite abusive terms by Augustine, who insisted that what might appear to be our free decisions were not free, but produced by corruption God had instilled in us. If we were to do anything good, it would only be because of a special injection of grace from the Lord. Augustine insisted on this so vociferously that not only were Pelagius's views finally condemned as heresy by the Council of Carthage in 417, when the two men were both dodderers of about 60, but he developed from this his interesting notion of the eternal damnation of unbaptized infants, for in the case of such children there would have been no time for the powerful background world to pierce through into ours, and, by touching them, give them a chance of a better fate. In time the Church moderated Augustine's view, though it carried on in Calvin and Luther. Today it's said to remain in near pure form only in their two most enthusiastic contemporary followers – Bible Belt Americans, the South African Boers – but as we shall see, it spreads further than that.

It turns out Pelagius himself was writing within an important, and ancient tradition, and one that is seen especially well in the way Homer handled this contact between the two worlds. It is worth looking at in some detail. His vision of the two realms starts off in the usual way. There are we scurrying mortals down here, trying this and attempting that, and there are also the gods, up there:

In the bright hall of Zeus upon Olympus.

They have absolute control over us, but it is not the control you might think. This is where Homer gets interesting. Only some of the time do they reach out to shake, thrash, blow off course, or otherwise directly influence individuals down here. More frequently there is another way. The fate which works through the world we are surrounded by of material objects, of boulders and seas and crops and weather – that is only one constraint on what we do. There is also the obligation of the feelings we have towards each other. Those are crucial for a human life. Without them we would be animals, not men.

With fate working by human obligation, we become, at least temporarily, free of any worry about our own will. The necessity of objects, and the necessity of human relations, both follow appropriate rules. Caught within either, we can just slide along. There is no need to second guess ourselves since the Gods are acting by standards of human relations, embedded in others, which we only have to contact. Augustine's subsequent Saints are tight-lipped and inhuman like SAS killers, because both are propelled by a force from the other world acting within them. It's as if a hypodermic from above the clouds reached down and injected them with a high-pressure squirt of grace. Homer's heroes are a more likeable bunch, because for them the force pulls, via human obligations, from without. It is the difference between the image of biplane pilots – thoughtful, gallant, with emotions of humor or defiance showing through their jaunty goggles – and that of jet fighter pilots: harsh and conditioned, eyes narrowed behind their visors, constrained by dials and display screens and pressurization levels, no place for humans, or obligations, or feeling.

This is why the reception of strangers is so important in the *Odyssey*. Consider what happens the day after Odysseus is flung ashore on Skheria Island. This, in the real time of the story (as opposed to all the flashbacks), is the first meeting Odysseus has with another human being. He has just spent two days in the sea, is naked and battered, and it is not surprising that when he bursts out from the bushes and advances on the serving maids by the stream:

Streaked with brine, and swollen, he terrified them, so that they fled, this way and that.

But Nausikaa, the King's adolescent daughter out with the serving maids, stands her ground. Now it's clear what Delta Force types or Augustine's men would do with this opportunity. They would leap forward and grap the girl in a merciless karate hold, threatening to throttle her unless she guided them to a boat. Their obligation is to take care of themselves while getting on with their mission, and that's it. Not so Odysseus. He is the master tactician, after all, and knows that would not do in Homer's world. Rather, keeping his distance he describes his lack of human support, which she will then be obligated to fill. This is the famous declaration:

Mistress, do me a kindness!
After much weary toil, I come to you,
and you are the first soul I have seen – I know
no others here. Direct me to the town.

From bushes to the City is the right direction. Nausikaa chides her maids:

Stay with me! Does the sight of a man scare you? . . .
No: this man is a castaway, poor fellow;
we must take care of him. Strangers and beggars
come from Zeus: a small gift, then, is friendly.

He is from the Other Side, but, unlike an SAS-type intruder – who would be autonomous, carrying all sources of energy in himself – he must be energized by us. He is passive, and our obligations to every other human being are what will here pull him along to the next step. The incursions of the gods are a test, a drawing-out, of our decency – not a rip in our world revealing a fiery realm of fate from which assaulters against us will emerge.

Where does this leave Odysseus's own will? He is free from second-guessing and responsibility, being pulled along now by the procedures Nausikaa sets up for him. But he is not free entirely. He has an obligation, too: he must stay in the realm where obligations remain clear. This means, for the poor man, no sex. It is difficult for Odysseus: he has had a long sojurn in the sea, he is now surrounded by lots of unaccompanied women, and, to make it worse, to show just what the temptation is which Odysseus must choose not to take,

Homer precedes the scene with a classic Mills and Boon account of
Nausikaa and the girls before Odysseus arrives: first-working up a
sweat with their washing, then going skinny dipping together in the
stream, and then rubbing olive oil into each other's naked bodies in
the sun. This is steamy in any age. (Also teenage Nausikaa has been
thinking it's about time she found a husband). It gets worse when the
freshly oiled maids lead Odysseus back to the stream, and invite him
to drop that olive branch he is holding and step in to bathe away his
brine. Does the great Odysseus sweat? Do his arms tremble, his
resolutions flag, and his more basic spirits rise? They do not. We can
almost hear the catch in his throat, as he gasps out:

> **'Maids', he said, 'keep away a little; let me
> wash the brine from my own back.'**

He must, because if he succumbs to the setting and mood, he will be
out of the realm of cool calculation. And you cannot have predictable
obligations when passion enters in. It is one, or the other. It is not the
particular moment of sex. That doesn't matter. It is the loss of
thought-out consequences that counts. You can't expect others to do
as they should, if you go ahead and do just what you want. Thrillers
or films which have commando heroes are not noted for the delicacy
in their intimate scenes. Passion and broad foresight do not go
together. Odysseus has to get that boat off the island; the girls, and the
breaking of restraint they and Nausikaa suggest, will have to be
foregone.

> **I take no bath, however, where you can see me –
> naked before young girls with pretty braids.**

Let us hope it was a cold stream.
   What about those who do break the obligations? Homer is not so
naive as to suppose that they didn't exist. They do, and if prevalent
would destroy everything. It's not just sex: any breaking of the
accepted standards of mutual, and rationally ascertainable, obligations will do it. Fate, which works through that network of
controlled obligations, would become powerless. Human society,
which also depends on controlled obligations, would be gone. This
would make a mockery out of Homer's world, his basic constructs,
the linkage between the two realms he assumes. It is intolerable for
Homer; it was intolerable for the civilized pagan Mediterranean

world he was a part of. It is the weakness of this, one of the very few possible models for any society. The breakers of obligation must be punished, and memorably. This they are.

First, just a hint, is the incident with Kyklops. He lives alone and is kind only to animals, which is wrong for a start, and then when Odysseus comes out with his usual statement of misfortune and request for comradely aid, Kyklops replies by throwing two of Odysseus's men on the cave floor, breaking their skulls and eating their bones, crunching as he goes. This is not generous. This shows a lack of compassion. This shows that trust, and the working of obligations through trust, cannot exist. There's only one thing for it. There will be no more Mr. Nice Guy from Odysseus. When the time comes to escape he does not just stab Kyklops in the eye. Rather, as Homer informs us with satisfaction, he

1 Rams the log into Kyklop's eye,
2 Turns it like a drill,
3 Pierces the eyeball till the roots pop out, and
4 Makes it hiss, like a hot axe in cold water.

That was just for beginners. Later on in the narrative comes a time when Odysseus is justified in getting really angry: this is the scene with his wife's suitors. They have violated the two key standards. They have abused the obligation of human need, because they gatecrashed Odysseus's home, lounging around and eating his food, even though they had plenty of property of their own. And they have also abused the obligation of staying in the predictable, ascertainable network of human clarity, because they lusted after Odysseus's wife, and did so openly. For this they get the arrows punching up through their throats, the spears driving clear through their chests, the broadswords lopping through limbs and heads until:

> Odysseus looked around him, narrow-eyed,
> for any others who had lain hidden
> while death's black fury passed . . .

And this from the same man who refused even to play footsie with Nausikaa.

Now although Odysseus was implacable in the Great Hall, it was for the one moment only. Unlike today's admired implacable killers, he is just scraping off the rough bits from a world where fate, when it does speak, is to do so by pulling men along passively through the network of obligations and trust. That's why the *Odyssey* ends not with the lopping and hacking, but two chapters later, out in the country, with Odysseus making a clear point of not slaughtering the relatives of the suitors. His responsibilities to those people, who themselves have done him or the system no evil, must be the helpful responsibilities he would have to any human.

IV.   COMMANDOS EMERGENT

We, today, have lost that habit of obligation. Our age, as that of so many others, is one where, especially across borders, even the hope of trust, community and equitability is gone. It is not just street crime, the sort of thing we know Odysseus or Nausikaa would suffer if flung ashore naked and battered in the South Bronx. It is more pervasive than that. Consider the fate of Odysseus washed up naked and battered, but still alive, before an immigration officer in almost any major port. He would not be knifed or coshed, as in a city: he would just be coolly returned to the sea which was killing him.

There have come to be too many times in this century when people have been treated merely as some sort of curious creature, with the form of humans, but somehow not really being human, and so lacking human needs which we would then be obliged to fulfil. The killing with little unease of several hundred thousand black-skinned individuals in the Congo by the Belgians as well as the other colonial slaughters acted out, a few years before the event, the slaughter with similarly little unease in the First World War of several million infantry soldiers by their superior officers, who sent them out into No Man's Land, where there were only bullets, barbed wire, and mines in the mud. It was the world of Kyklops's cave, our era somehow locked inside it, all residents accordingly reduced to the fury of Odysseus in that ahuman realm. After the First World War, this treatment was hard to escape. Those infantry soldiers, dressed in identical cotton material, registered with multi-digit code numbers, shepherded in screaming groups across the barbed wire, occurred again twenty-five years later, with other bodies, other wire. What feeling was there from German towards Jew to fling him there? What feeling do we have towards the Russian child whom we will consider burning to death with hydrogen bombs if his government opposes ours?

Our answer has been the fantasy of Delta Force and the SAS. They are what we are left with, when trust of each other is gone. There still are the two worlds of background force and scurrying men as in Homer, but the link-up, when it comes, is not the pulling of community, but the pushing of individual assertion. It was the attitude behind that rumor, quickly believed and spread through Europe and America, that German soldiers dressed as nuns were being used in the 1940 invasion of the Netherlands. The rumor became so widespread because everyone knew what it meant. The real problem was not columns of infantry in drag, but an order violation much closer to home. What we trust more than all else, a pure, white-dressed, virgin in our community, was in this case not going to trust back. Instead she was going to pull out a sub-machinegun and kill, we perhaps recognizing the giveaway beard stubble on her cheek only as we fell. It was a summary of the fact that nothing could be trusted in that era, because all the treats of community and the progress we were supposed to share in, all the wonders of large organization and high-tech and airplanes, were being used against us. Thus Orwell's upset at those highly civilized human beings flying overhead in machines, trying to kill us; an upset that held even though in most countries early in the Second World War civilian deaths from air attack were negligible as a percentage of the total population.

The result?

Hell is other people.

(Sartre's *No Exit*, 1977).

It was exactly in this period that the vision of implacable commandos began to take off. It was the popularization of paratroopers, Chindits, SAS, SBS, Rangers, and marine commandos: hard, autonomous, man-machine all. The fact that those forces had little decisive role in the Second World War, and almost always lost when confronted with the bureaucratic man-machine of massed regular troops, was not important. Since the community maintenance Homer needed was gone, these commandos had to be there to show another way. They showed life sensibly adapted to the Kylops' cave.

They are, accordingly, the individuals we turn to today. They have no will, for they are perfect – and you cannot will beyond perfection. It is divine. The infantries of post-Reformation Europe, however neatly wielded into masses under one general's rule, were not divine, but just a demonstration of what happens when God's plenum has been secularized, following Newton, into a self-sustaining clockwork entirely on This Side. The SAS-man, however, still gets his squirting hypodermic transfusion direct from the Other Side. This is not to say that he is never good. If I were on a hijacked plan I would be very happy to see him storming aboard. It's just the insistent praising of him in civilian life, and for whatever action he is used, that is disappointing.

It is a return to the solution of Augustine. His men were on a mission too. Who can torture with a straight face? Augustine, Calvin and their saints, of course, for the individual they are torturing is already damned while they, the tormentors, have that injection of individual grace. It genuinely gives strength: revolutionaries will often get up before others awake, eager for the day's struggle. The power from the Other Side, the backdrop world, wells through the believer. Commando missions are especially good for getting injections of grace or energy from the Other Side, since because such missions end in killing or transfixion of another human, then that human certainly hadn't been contacted with grace – just as required for Augustine's scheme to hold.

Military weapons such as missiles or Star Wars lasers are these killers *par excellence*. They're emotionless, automatic, and work by inner necessity, without concern of others' needs or interest. That's why governments so easily pass contracts to pay for them. That's also why civil servants and journalists so often get excited when dealing with them – feel that they're being lifted out of the ordinary – while they feel bored, in the humdrum, when dealing with civilian projects. The shiny military goods really are special: they're objects that have received that hypodermic injection of grace, direct from the Other Side. By surrounding ourselves with them and their minutiae we really do get to immerse ourselves in the world of grace and specialness – in the sacred, satisfying clear world of the Other Side.

This is why nobody likes SAS-type missions which will leave humans on the receiving end not dead, not transfixed or held down, but capable of independent and possibly even improved action. Who could get excited about sending a force of thousands of healthy, trained and implacable Delta Force men to rebuild our central cities? If they did succeed, then the objects of their mission would have been proven to be not damned, and so they, the doers, would have lost the force of being saints in touch with the beyond. What kind of a fantasy is that? Send them to the Falklands or Libya, however, and all is well. If we must keep our fantasies away from official military missions, then the object will have to be something else without divine grace, something else clearly non-blessed such as the rocks or rivers or other geological formations our commando-like best climbers or kayak teams battle against. That, at least, can be the moral equivalent of war.

It's true that there will be a certain fussing at this image's harshness, a certain amount of searching for individuals carried by fate who are pure and not damned. This is possibly what explains the efforts of some upper-middle-class citizens to live in tough working-class neighborhoods. There the locals, with their jolly ways, their automatic, unquestioning habits, are supposed to demonstrate causality, the God-force we have so much trouble with, coming out pure. But such slumming is a refinement only a minority indulge in. More common is to depend on our pure, unadulterated individual machine-men; to admire the scrambling jets; the efficient, internally driven, and so free marvels. These weapons and commandos are our heroes, because them we can trust. They cut through fate, because they have one obligation only.

And that's a killer.

Part Two
In America

4
Creating the *New York Times*

I was in New York for the first time in a while the other day when a young woman came up to me and said: 'I want to pay taxes.' Perhaps I had misheard, I thought, but no, she went on doggedly: 'Please! I want to be a taxpayer.' This was interesting. I've paid taxes for years but never really wanted to. Yet this woman was insistent.

There was nothing I could do to help, so I left her and walked on a bit more. Another woman piped up. 'I decided', she called out, that 'I needed a change.' A change? Yes. 'Instead of going the right way, I went the wrong way.' Now she was on the right track, though, she told me; 'I have the courage and self-confidence' to get to the end.

As the streets were proving so odd I strolled inside the Manhattan House of Detention. There it was cool, and maybe I could find an official to talk to. But after being inside just a few minutes I stopped dead. In front of me was a strapping 22-year-old, with a leopard tattooed on his bicep, and St. Raphael emblazoned on his forearm. It looked dangerous. He stared at me, then spoke.

'Most of the problems I hear are family problems.' He was a hardened prisoner who had volunteered as an inmate observation aide. If he spotted abnormal behavior he knew what to do. 'You talk to the inmate gently, explaining that depression can pass.' It is a gentle approach, and apparently it works. 'All the men know they can talk to me', he said, quiet yet proud.

These heartening stories do not come from a random walk in New York City, of course, but rather from a random walk in the *New York Times* (quotes from articles from July 21, 1985, pp. 37, 39 and 35.) It is an altogether different place. In New York City people get mugged, stabbed, raped, have their wishes thwarted, dodge their taxes, stay on the wrong path, suffer from overcrowding, kill each other in prison, have heartless bosses, and are surrounded by unfriendly, incoherent and usually menacing human beings. In the *New York Times* there is none of that. Most inhabitants of that paper, if they are Americans, speak in full sentences, try to get on, go out of their way to pay taxes, and do not menace, rape, stab or otherwise thwart their fellow man.

Why does the paper go to such lengths to show what isn't true? It's not just lies, evasions, a lauding of New York or the Sulzbergers (the publishers), but rather a systematic, and most odd, approach to reality.

Well, the image of Two Cities – a cruel and messy one we live in, a clean and ideal one which we would prefer to live in – is just another reworking of our old Other Side notion; what in the west has been especially influential through St. Augustine's accounts of the City of God, and the City of Man.

For Augustine it was allowable that the City of Man could be in such terrible shape, because before too long the millenium would arrive and those few lucky believers who had an injection of grace from the holy would be hoisted up to a City of God come true. But few of us believe this any more. Heaven has crashed, and landed on earth. We can't be content being unhappy down here for the sake of a future promise up there, not when the Up There no longer exists. But how to make us happy? With heaven around it was easy, you could just promise everybody what they wanted. But today? Somehow the solace, the sources of happiness, have to be found – people demand that wherever they're living. And yet, trying to find the solace entirely down here, on This Planet, is no easy job. People have different desires, different jobs and expectations and ways of talking and everything. How can they all be made to fit together and yet not feel thwarted?

Intelligent beings watching us from a distant planet would have seen humans dance around many different replacement Bibles in the search for that solace. At one time it would have been the crowds listening to a shrieking Robespierre; in another place and time solemn Moscow schoolchildren pondering the texts of Marxist-Leninism. Today, to understand the answer accepted over a large part of the earth's surface, they could just focus their telescopes on one most curious individual, the middle-aged professional New Yorker, stretched out on the couch of his Brooklyn apartment, 7.30a.m. and his morning's coffee already brewing in the next room, an early hot buttered bagel on the plate beside him, and, most importantly, perched comfortably on his belly, that huge mass of reconstituted wood shavings he is looking forward to browsing in before breakfast; *The New York Times*. It isn't just for the news stories – who ever remembers all the news stories? – but rather for something deeper, something more soothing, something that precisely through its skill at showing what isn't entirely true can still make sense of his life within the merged Two Cities that make up his planet now, perpetually having to wonder how he and everyone else should get along.

He won't be the only reader of the paper this morning, there will be others in his city and across the country, including many much more wealthy. There will also be other papers on offer, tabloids far inferior, which we will have to look at later. But for now let us join the distant outer space creatures looking just at this man, keeping watch even as he sits up startled from the couch, and races to the kitchen where the coffee is bubbling over, in his haste leaving the crumpled paper behind; let us join them, with their Super X-Ray telescope, and examine more closely this document he has left behind. It can't be a detailed look, just broad outlines at this distance, but still enough, perhaps, to start explaining what's going on.

II.   MARRIAGE: THE VERY RICH AND THE *NEW YORK TIMES*

We begin with the marriage listings: two pages, every Sunday, conveniently placed in the same spot of the second section. There seems to be much call for it. *New York Times* residents are fond of children ('He's such an affectionate child and so gentle', 21 July, 1985, p. 41), they are fond of each other ('Christa has a real keen way of dealing with people', p. 14), and sometimes *very* fond of each other ('It's so great to be here that I just want to hug these people', p. 47). And yet, somehow perversely, all these keen, friendly, fond people somehow never get down to the nitty-gritty. In all the rest of the paper there's no copulation, whether illicit or legally sanctioned, not even a hint of it: no lewd gazes, no reference to having kiddie-winkles, no proposals, marriage invitations, weddings, or other steps that might be thought biologically proper to individuals so enthusiastic about each other. All is barred, screened totally from the paper, for there is no reason for ordinary people to go ahead – and stop being ordinary.

Which is the key. The ordinary people in the *New York Times* are already busy enough striving, helping, being good, and otherwise getting along. Undergoing a biological change in addition would be too much. The individuals in the above examples were helping deprived city children, commenting on a lucky schoolteacher, and working in a writer's workshop respectively. Would they do that if they were busy mating?

For the 160 or so individuals each week whose children get listed on the marriage page however, it's different. There are no qualms about carnal biology for them: the page is littered with photos of young women looking, well, fertile and eager. It is a meat market – the one place where the *New York Times* gives way – but it is allowed because it is a special meat market. The women on display are not there as eager receptacles for just anyone. Money, on these pages, almost always marries money. At the top of the first column (July 21, 1985, p. 45) we meet Wendy Weil, granddaughter of the president of Macys, who is about to marry Richard Stockton Rush the Third, son of Richard Stockton Rush the Second, who was chairman of the Peregrine Oil and Gas Company in California. The listings continue in the same fresh style throughout.

These individuals get to have their pairings listed because for them and theirs the careful carrying on of power links is what counts. To give real oomph to such power links you can't have mere horizontal transfers, a sort of 'pass the pancake' among elderly millionaires sitting around the board table. Rather the links must be extended into the future, a capsule tossed across the barriers of time. Only one way is yet known to do this – sex within carefully controlled groups – which is why the *New York Times* descends on this page to intimations of the hot and sweaty among these carefully dealt out heirs.

It doesn't fit in with the tone of the rest of the paper – indeed staff journalists have been known to grumble about its even being there. But that doesn't matter. The very rich are earthling's commandos. Like Delta Force men or the SAS, watching them in action shows a strange and powerful Other Side being revealed. For real commandos it is a realm of pure necessity and destruction. For the very rich it is a world of money and extreme, unjustified power. The difference is that while many citizens get a pleasure out of seeing the fiery world from which commandos come, the revealing of the very rich on these pages is something of an accident. It just shows up because the biggest winners in the earthly city demand this promise of immortality, and in the society marriage pages, however it may jar, they're damned well going to get it. The problem is that, left alone, this would appear as a most irritating floating City of God, hovering like Gulliver's Laputa, far above the reach of the ordinary *New York Times* reader. And on the planet where he has to live, where he's come to believe that what he wants has to be granted down on earth or else he has no chance of getting it ever, that would just be too unpleasant a reminder to have. How is the problem fixed?

The private schools the kids being married went to are pretty bad, all those Hotchkisses and Grotons that most Americans can't afford, but at least as soon as they're done there the youngsters go out and do some work. The woman we met earlier who was so keen to pay her taxes might be upset if she was folded onto this page and saw that the wealthy newly-weds will now lie indolently in the sun in Palm Springs till they die. But when she finds out that they are investment consultants, publishing assistants, law firm associates? Then they're just like her; just going back to the swirling rush of ordinary life that the rest of the paper's subjects have been immersed in all this time. The indiscreet interlude of the biological hot and heavy is passed over: it was a rip in the stage backdrop, a peek up through a gap in the clouds, that now, through this evidence of goods works, and after just the briefest of glimpses, will be sewn over.

Even the moment of that indiscretion was handled in a way not to too terribly offend anyone. Did the marriage announcement say that Ms. Weil could not resist Mr. Rush any more? That she was embarrassing herself, neglecting her job ('Miss Weil . . . is an account manager with Ladd Associates in San Francisco, a consultant to magazine publishers'), moping and groaning until those blessed moments of the day when *he* would phone? It did not. Rather Ms. Weil and the thirty-nine other young ladies on the marriage page went through the pairing up process just as atom-like particles would, sliding emotionless, automatically, from one slot in the world – Princeton and publishing – to another slot: Princeton, publishing . . . and Mrs. Richard Rush. This is what everyone wants in a democracy. It's like Chicago's late vote-rigging Mayor Daley doing his dirty work but then having the decency to wait in line to vote just like anyone else. The marriage announcements show that in whatever they do, even what could be the most intimate and private, the very rich are following rules just like any other good professional would. There's no conspiracy in things working out this neatly. It's just a convenient convergence, that only looks so suspiciously neat because we are watching this particular planet, which has in fact developed it. But more on neat overlaps later.

III. SELF-ADVANCEMENT: BLUE COLLAR AND THE *NEW YORK TIMES*

If there's this occasional weak spot in the *New York Times*, imagine how much worse the unevenness in America could seem to ordinary

working guys. To them the relatively pampered and opportunity-
rich lives of the average *New York Times* readers, there displayed in
the real world all around them, in their bosses and on TV and at the
nice shops; those are even more of an easily spied and irritating realm
than the mating rituals of the very rich were to the *New York Times*
readers themselves.

Sometimes the irritation does get too much, whence the purported
answer by the head of Macy's to Rupert Murdoch's request that the
store put more ads in what was then Murdoch's *New York Post*:

But Rupert, your readers are our shoplifters.

But far more often the non *New York Times* readers don't think of
shoplifting or taking what isn't theirs. There's not even political
hatred. The goings on in the wealthier, comfortable middle-class
world around them which could be so irritating are accepted. Peace is
maintained. How is this second covering over carried out?

The ultimate answer in America is a trust in an improved future,
and the feeling of many blue-collar and lower-middle-class families
that they're only holding their lowly positions temporarily. Certainly when growth slows down and that promise doesn't get
fulfilled, relations have become rough. But still, even when people
are expecting a better future, something still has to be done to ensure
harmony now, while they do happen to be in those inferior positions.
And this something is a habit of thinking which hooks everything
that happens, all the strange and potentially irritating events in the
world out there, back to items that we already know and feel
comfortable with. Thus when the *New York Times* headlines

Dow Tops 2,000 for the First Time
As Wall St. Extends Latest Rally (January 9, 1987)

which could be irritating, a reminder of the hoity-toity good thing
the *New York Times* types are in on, a look at the *New York Post* shows
that it's saying, on the same day:

WOW! POW! DOW! 2002: A STOCK ODYSSEY

Wrapped up that way the stock market advance is not irritating,
strange, surprising. It reminds readers of the '2001' film title, which
they already know; it fits in with the joke phrasing 'Wow, Pow,

Zow' which they know already too. It has cleaved off the familiar, from the strange and dangerous things out there in the mist. Nothing escapes this so–easy–to–wield conceptual Excalibur:

One, two! One, two! And through and through
The vorpal blade went snicker-snack!

Great chunks of stuff fall on the inside, on their side, and once they're there the readers can be quite at ease about them. Down-market journalists go out to hunt, grab strange things, make them familiar and then heave them over the wall into the conceptual stockade where the readers of their papers live.

The approach is not exclusively American. For while the middle class approach differs considerably from country to country, it's interesting that this one working class attitude has come to be accepted, with little variation, world-wide – yet another sign of the limited diversity down there. (It makes the jobs of the international press magnates easier, too.) Consider that incident touched on back in Chapter 3, where Reagan in 1985 ordered four American military jets to surround a plane carrying four Palestinians from Egypt and divert them to Italy. On the face of it that was a complex act, involving abstruse and distant political authorities, and machines functioning on the basis of technology hardly anyone understood. But the British tabloid press, as much as the American, made it into something else. All that happened, according to London's *Sun*, was that 'Rambo Reagan' (p. 1 headline) pulled off a 'Rambo-style raid' (news story, p. 4). That is better. That is familiar. That is something everyone knows about and can understand.

The language in the *Sun*'s report was composed almost entirely of clichés – in the first two paragraphs we come across the phrases 'pulled off [a] raid', 'mighty blow', 'brilliant capture', 'getting away with murder', 'hailed as a triumph' – which again readers were used to and had seen before. The linking words between the clichés came from ordinary conversation, being primarily single syllables; and to make the whole event more normal the *Sun* noted that it began in 'a Chicago bakery on Thursday', which is as clear, specific and eminently graspable an origin as can be.

Many popular papers not only compared the event to a specific movie, but went on to describe it as the sort of movie or television film readers will have seen many times before. Thus in the *Daily Express* (p. 1):

**It was 8:20 p.m. London time. Time to act. Mr.
Reagan speaking by air-to-ground telephone alert-
ed his top aides in the White House.
     Then his 'Go get 'em' command was flashed to
the skipper of the U.S. carrier Saratoga . . .**

The curious and unique conjuncture of men, machines, and authority
in the air over the Mediterranean one night in October was accounted
for. Who had to worry about oil companies and arms sales and White
House jockeyings for power and the real terror of the poor tourists on
the Achille Lauro? All were events that had been pulled from the
threatening and barely understood outside, where everything that
howls and shrieks and murders exists, and transformed to be lugged
into the good side, the tabloid reader's *own* side, where everything is
safe, and warm, and above all familiar.

   What has been pulled into the most known, into the 'us', is
something that no one is then going to feel irritated about. In
particular, the goodies that those potentially hoity-toity *New York
Times* types get to be in on are not going to be irritating. They will be
hauled in too, made to appear as stereotypes, oddities of higher
income lifestyle which have been seen so many times that they don't
hurt, don't grate, but just strike one set of familiar chords among
others deep inside blue collar readers, deep where trust and familiarity
and comfortableness reign. The tabloid reader, looking around him
on the subway, seeing a blur of different characters, many showing
clearly by their dress or expressions that they are in a higher or more
interesting life, can just apply these ready-made, comfortable
hauling-in stereotypes. He can even develop new stereotypes as he
goes, since the tabloids have granted him the tool of being able to see
not individual individuals, but general individuals. It's an easy tool –
what the mediaevals called category realism – to imitate: this older
gentleman will become All Trustworthy Bankers, this younger
woman with the leather agenda book will become Another Dynamic
Young Businesswoman. Who's going to feel like complaining, to feel
that something wrong or irritating is going on around them when
there only are such cozily well-known individuals there to see?

   Throughout the mass circulation papers this approach is taken.
Again there was no need for any great conspiracy. Some early
newspapers attempting mass circulation, such as those of Harmsworth or Hearst, latched on to this approach, and their papers
prospered. Others missed it, and failed. If no one had found it there

would be a different world to see. Maybe it would be the one where
WASPs slave on the plantations; or perhaps the one where there are
ceremonial executions of the three leading stockholders each month.
All we can say is that the modern west is a place where the 'pulling
into the familiar' approach *was* offered, and was accepted; helped by
the fact that it's a warm and cozy approach: that reaching inside of
laboring citizens to reinforce the innermost, most cherished parts –
exactly the parts they like to think of as what God pays attention to.
Also it made sense of the working class readers' lives, where
venturing out of the stockade of the familiar, into the world of
advancement and new careers, may have been greatly desired, but in
fact was not able to be frequently done. Leaving the raw outside
world on offer, not doubled back by deft presentation to appear as
part of the usual and familiar, would have been an unpleasant
reminder of this lack of movement. That way revolutions lay.

It's a smooth image, the blue collar accepting the middle class, the
middle class accepting the rich, but has a terrible problem with
dynamism. Everybody staying neatly in order should produce the
passive, stagnant life of a communist country, or an old European
kingdom. But America is not passive and stagnant. At least one of its
groups must have the right to produce something new, a lot of
something new. It is not hard to tell which one this will be.

Compare the faces of the tabloid and *New York Times* readers.
Most of the time the down-market paper readers will be at ease, used
to their journalist hunters coming back with these most incredible
objects safely pinioned in their columns of type. You see truckers at a
diner or salesgirls at lunch, turn, blasé and with a yawn, from a page
with a glaring black headline promising Shock! and Horror! It's not
troublesome for them. They've been watching the returning hunters
with their Shocking and Horrible finds for years. It's all being made
part of the familiar, worked in with slangy headlines and emotions all
can identify with. After the readers put down the paper they can go
back to their work, the same old rule-following job, untroubled.

Not so the *New York Times* reader. When, finally, he goes through
his paper at his morning breakfast table, unfurling it over the half-
finished bagel, his lips are likely to be slightly pursed, the paper will be
held high, and from this posture he will emit 'ohs' or 'hmmms' or
other attentive-marking sounds, so showing that what he's finding in
there is a range of interesting data, any one of which might bear
thinking about. The *New York Times* reader has to be such a glancing,

assessing, evaluating reader. For he is not just reading but actually
going on scouting hunts in the paper, clucking and wryly commenting as he pokes around. For him there is an extensive background
terrain to study down there, and odd characters political or human on
display, scurrying around anxiously on trail bikes in that terrain being
sensible — seeing the over-pitted or dead-end trails to be avoided as
well as we do – or not. The *New York Times* reader scanning his paper
at the breakfast table is in a helicopter over a huge unmarked desert
trail road system, watching a muddy and thorn-scratched Yahoo or
foreign politician or simply a businessman on a motorcycle trying to
get out.

   If they don't make it, if they're doing something wrong, the reader
doesn't point down on the columns of newsprint and guffaw, great
rollicking belly-laughs, enough to make the helicopter shake, and the
maze-runner look up startled. That's low class. The *New York Times*
is much milder with failures than the popular papers. Rather all the
proper *New York Times* reader shows is disappointment. He will take
a sip of fresh coffee and just give a minute shake of his head to distance
himself, a symbolic shrug for the poor lost sap.

   The reason is that he knows that just as soon as he puts down the
paper and sets off to work, he will be racing on the equivalent of this
dusty and uncharted terrain himself, pulling on his helmet and having
to kick-start his own trail bike's engine. It is what he has been doing
for years. First there was choosing his original career, then all the
problems of keeping it going upward by selecting among all the
intriguing but terribly unclear possibilities of transfer or promotion
on offer, and now, even within one job, he still has to choose the right
approach in each phone call, memo, business decision.

   It is an important role. The *New York Times* readers haven't laid
out the country and its opportunity roads; that's a prerogative of big
money. But they're not the poor shleps who serve as the wheels or
suspension bearings that are smacking directly on to the dirt either;
that's the popular paper readers. They are, simply, the nice man in the
business suit gingerly grasping the bike's handles, who has to work
the throttle, select the right turnings, and notice where the hundreds
of thousands of other competing *New York Times* types, bouncing
apprehensively on their motorbikes, are going too. Sometimes
roaring past them all will be an exceptionally ambitious driver in a
low-slung Ferrari, tearing out to the horizon and perhaps, if he's very
good, up and away into society-marriage-page heaven. But that's
rare, and actually not too upsetting. The bumpety-bump jouncing on

the ordinary, only slightly souped-up trail bikes has a certain fun, it gives the readers more independence than most other positions do, and it also really does give America that energy, that constant homing in on opportunities, which hardly any other countries do as well.

IV.   CONSEQUENCES AND CONSOLATIONS

What personality do you get in the different roles? (In real life of course almost everyone is a mix, responding at some time to the pull of either side.) The main delight of the tabloid reader's side, the one great advantage of life down there, is that it's easy to hook up to other people close to him, to feel that they're sharing his feelings very, very closely. There is no embarrassment here. In just one day's issue of the *New York Post* there is:

KIDNEY GIRL'S MOM: THANK YOU, POST READERS

UPPER WEST SIDERS: DON'T BRING DOWN CURTAIN ON THE THALIA

GRIEVING MOM: THEY'LL NEVER FIND MY DIANE

(All *New York Post* from January 9, 1987)

This is telepathy! The innermost feelings of all these individuals are being made clear, extracted out, put on immediate, direct display outside for everyone to share. Characters in a Woody Allen film would find such headlines coarse. But what are his characters doing except trying to make contact across human barriers themselves? They fail because it's a huge jump from the attitudes in their ordinary lives to do so. But in the tabloid press, as in the expectations of the tabloid reader, it's just what should happen. He sees another person, and immediately shares his feelings; it's like a little transistor radio he has swallowed coming on.

Against this one huge satisfaction, this warmth and apparently direct contact, there is the equally huge lacking that there is no way to get out of the present tense in which it works. The down-market journalists are busy creatures, stripped to the waist as they strain and sweat and connive to haul in big chunks of reality each day – but there is one great part of the terrain they never hunt in: the past, or the future. It's trefe, verboten. Everything they provide just 'is':

GIANT STEP!
     by Hank Gola
**The Giants are going to the Super
Bowl!
The Giants are going to the Super
Bowl!
The Giants are going to the Super
Bowl!**

(*New York Post*, January 12, 1987)

The words here, even the emotion, are all suspended in a deathly void. It is a single blip of activity on an otherwise black and infinitely stretching oscilloscope screen; an existence caught, forever, in the single narrow dot of the continuous present.

There is a terrible isolation in that, not from one's immediate friends, that stays safe, but from everything beyond that, from any possible basis for the tabloid reader to understand his life. Where do things come from? Where do they go? This he will never know. The approach doesn't allow it. Everything the journalist hunters trap and bring in – the rapes and scandals and football victories – are just fleeting items of the present. The reader falls into it because it matches his job and life, where orders and most everything else are bluntly given, but still no one can be happy with an existence that isolated time.

This makes for a lot of anger in politics. Someone who offers a different political vision than the one he's used to is insulting him in a terrible way. The politician/seer is up on a peak or a tower, looking all around, yelling down what he sees of the past or the future from up there. In America this generally comes out at full strength only in times of crisis or close to an election, but in Britain, where there is such a rigid class system, this attitude can be seen all the time.

Back in 1985, as one example, one of Prime Minister Thatcher's Cabinet ministers, Peter Walker, said that her policies hadn't worked and the country was turning against her. He had brought in the past to foretell the future. The British down-market newspapers accordingly could not rebut what he said. Even if he was wrong, even if the past had been very, very nice and the future was going to be rosy beyond belief, they couldn't say so. It would be, as Russell remarked in a different context, like telling a man with a remarkably large nose that when you speak of noses you except those that are unduly large. This is not a pleasant way of dealing with a painful topic. It would have been admitting that the future and past were where readers should look to solve their problems.

Walker had done the unpardonable, the unmentionable, and so the British tabloids had to rebut not his ideas, but *him*, his existence. That is what Mr. Murdoch's immensely popular (London) *Sun* newspaper, circulation over four million, did in its leading editorial (October 12, 1985). First of all it declared that Walker didn't have long to exist:

> **If he feels he could do better, why**
> **doesn't he stand against Mrs. Thatcher**
> **for the leadership of the party now as**
> **he is perfectly entitled to do?**
> **Because he knows he would be totally**
> **humiliated.**

Secondly it took a pleasure jeering at his failure, watching him be driven out of existence:

> **We've got news for him. Mrs. Thatcher**
> **ain't going just yet, not for a long time.**
> **And when she finally does, it won't**
> **be the over-ambitious Mr Walker**
> **who steps into her shoes.**

Finally it showed that when he does cease to exist it will be fitting:

> **. . . We suggest he join the ex-Cabinet**
> **moaning minnies on the back benches.**

The present had been cleaned up, and the ideas of cause in past and future left untouched. The reader may recollect American conversations about politics which show a similar uneasiness with anything except the same annihilation.

Crammed into the present tense, the tabloid reader's personal emotions are going to come out strongly too. On January 9, 1987, when the *New York Times* coolly observed in a headline:

> **Judge Overturns**
> **A Ruling Limiting**
> **Milk Sales In City**

the *New York Post* was gushing (in red capitals):

HOLY COW! WE WON!

What else were they going to say? Legal rulings are things that extend back in time, that stretch forward into the future too, and the *Post* reader is just not used to concerning himself with that. All that's left is his feeling about the event now.

This makes life difficult whenever he feels thwarted. He can't easily think back into the past to consider the origins of a problem, the source of what's bothering him. Nor is he going to be used to speculating ahead, vividly thinking out the future time-course of a problem, so that he can hold his feeling in reserve, on ice, while he waits for the best moment to inject his response. Instead, suddenly it all just pours out, now: there is a lot of expressed anger, sudden eruptions of yelling and hate, in these readers' lives.

The tabloids goad their readers along in this. They insist that it is right, normal, appropriate to have these emotional surges, and to let them rip out. It happens with ordinary people: all those individuals in their pages bursting out into rape, beatings, murder, revenge. It happens with respectable people too: all those film stars being silly and emotional, even clerics here surge with emotion:

O'CONNOR HITS BACK
**Slams Jewish Critics
of his peace efforts**

is how the *Post* (January 12, 1987) reports the archbishop of New York feeling on his return from a Mideast trip. How angry the archbishop actually was is hard to tell, only he would know, but there were other ways to present it. In the *New York Times* vision it was merely:

O'CONNOR IS UPSET
**BY CRITICS OF TRIP
Says he is disappointed . . .**

Someone stuck in the tabloid life can either struggle, or accept it. Struggling means trying to work his way up, into a better job, where he's not stuck just taking orders. But accepting it is also common, and means wallowing in television, whipping himself up enthusiastically to be a good buddy at the bar, cheering himself silly at a baseball game; and pushing to the back of his mind that nagging realization that all he's doing occurs in just one isolated, soon to vanish, floating blip in time.

Whether it can be pushed away entirely though is doubtful, for there is still one more item in all the tabloid papers, an oddity, an apparent exception to the tone of all the other pages, but an exception which readership surveys show to be one of the items most certain to be read.

This is the astrology column. Astrology brings in the past, it brings in the future, and it shows how with just a little easy effort on the readers' own part – reading that astrology column – he can live out the links from the one to the other. It is an all-terrain vehicle: smashing through the pallistrades of the present-tense stockade, it mangles a couple of flabbergasted journalists in its path, and roars out into the woods.

It's fun, it's exciting, its liberating and shows adventure – but it doesn't really take the rider anywhere:

Eventful goings–on take place this weekend. People will be drawn to your positive vibes. You're almost too good to be true.

(*New York Daily News*, January 9, 1987, Pisces)

This is not new. This is not a surprise. This ('You're almost too good to be true') is just where he came from. Almost all the forecasts are like that: they start by confronting readers with the outside, they bring in tempting and intriguing events from the future, but then, instead of going out where they came from to answer them, instead of seeking historical or other causal roots, the forecasts give up, turn the reader back in on himself, and say that all he needs do to overcome them is more of what he has been or should have been doing all along. That is a long ride to get nowhere. It is a mad escape on an all-terrain vehicle . . . that gets routed to a U-turn and sent barrelling back into the prison grounds of the quarantined present it started from.

Even so there might still seem to be hope. Even if the solutions are simple there's still the basic point that astrology only works by assuming that everything is connected up, that there is an invisible but incredibly powerful network linking us with the moon and the stars and causality and the Secrets of the Universe and everything else that is big and powerful and important out there:

Find a nice quiet place for your romantic rendezvous this weekend. Whether you know it or not, your guardian angel is looking over your shoulder.

(*Ibid.*, Aries)

The Weekend edges in at a snail's pace . . . Moon is in Gemini. Your love life gets a royal shot in the arm.

(*Ibid.*, Gemini)

Which would be fine, which would light up the whole oscilloscope, connect his tiny blip of existence out to the very edges of knowledge . . . but for the fact that hardly anyone *really* believes in astrology. Certainly not powerful people:

I like to hear it. I like to hear what the hell it says, which is interesting. But I don't consult the Ouija board on very important problems. I ask, you know, what's the problem with my boat?

(Henry Ford II, in Robert Lacey, *Ford*, p. 655)

And even its daily readers will admit that although astrology might be true, it's not actually true-true, not true in the way that the rules for driving a car or balancing a checkbook or even having to follow a yelled order from their boss is true. It merely is true in the way that readers of the simple papers get to pretend an escape from their present is true. That's all. Everyone likes to have the basis of their life be supported by a standard they respect. But anyone who rests his hopes on astrology shows that he knows that standard is worthless. There's a deep sadness in this.

The *New York Times* reader doesn't have to pretend this way. His life is embedded in time, he gets to see the past and future, the real scientifically true past and future, and above all he gets the power to take control of his life. His newspaper doesn't give him that nonsense of astrology. No quality newspaper would do that. In the evolution of print forms, astrology was excluded from serious books and papers over three centuries ago. (Only the cartoon on the quality editorial pages, a direct holdover from the period of mediaeval symbolic art, shows what had been.) What the *New York Times* reader gets instead is his ride in the surveying helicopter of the editorial writers, where the expert pilot yells over the roar of the blades lots of advice, over a thousand words worth each morning, enough to describe the reader's own building, soon just a little slab lost in the distance, and yet still keep on describing, pointing out events all the way along the terrain, important political and economic events anyone venturing out will have to watch out for, events that would be totally out of sight, way over the horizon, if someone just stood up on tippy-toe and tried to spy them out of the breakfast-room window. And the reason they can't be seen any other way is that these are events that exist, not in the present tense, not in the usual world the reader experiences right around him, but in the conditional, especially the subjunctive conditional, in the realm of possibility and contingency and the assessing 'if-then'. For that is just what the *New York Times* reader needs in his life, a detailed distant map, not just showing the location of his first possible turn out there, but the *result* of taking that turn, what the roads look like after that, the whole terrain of alternate futures made clear – and that's what the editorial writers show.

That real choice, that ability to step back and plan a life, the reader gunning his trail-bike along the right roads to the City later, or up the right stairwell in the office building, is the one great advantage of the *New York Times* life, but it also contains the one great weakness. For being able to choose, living life in the subjective conditional where he's always considering what to do next, means that the particular item of the present he pushes into the equation to start the operation, the given chunk of this world he grabs to start the assessing: that chunk can never be grabbed with all the feeling that he has. How could he when it is but half the equation, merely the bit that he needs to start his assessing? That chunk, that immediate bit of the world around him, will be grabbed not for itself, but only for its use as a fulcrum into the future; it will be held, but – and this is the tragedy – it can only be held circumspectly, coolly, with self-awareness.

The personality this produces we know well. The proper *New York Times* reader will have a core thing at the center of his personality, some inner soul which contains all his deepest feelings and fears and desires, which he brings up close to the world, which he has slots on to place and examine items from that world, but which he feels it would be wrong to ever let be fully pulled out or revealed to that world. Since emotions are a sign of that inner thing coming out, emotions will have to be guarded against. If they do come out it is only an accident, a little bit that spurted up when he wasn't looking,

something that has kicked and struggled to try to get out but which, if
he is doing the right thing, he will be very careful to tie back in place:

Knicks ready to think about – gasp! – a playoff berth
(January 12, 1987)

If it ever did come fully out he would lose the crucial ability to step
back and choose. The *Post* reports that a

BIGAMY DOCTOR GOES A-COURTIN'
(January 9, 1987, p. 1)

This is a man who has some incredible lust for bigamy, some totally
uncontrollable need, so strong that he has turned into this monoman-
iacal thing called a Bigamy Doctor. For the rest of his life that is what
he will be. But the *New York Times* merely reports, calmly on an
inside page, that

A Manhattan doctor arrested on bigamy charges will probably not . . .

Here we have a man, who has kept his reason, who is still a Manhattan
doctor; who made one unfortunate choice perhaps, a little slip-up in
counting, but in the future can overcome it, forget that indiscretion,
and go back to his cool, successful doctoring.

The *New York Times* encourages such holding back wherever it
can. On the music page there are accounts of concerts which in theory
could be reported in a way to get the reader to stand up at his
breakfast table and shout, knocking the fresh orange juice over,
sending the coffee jug flying; the reader spreading his arms out and
bursting into song, hurrahing and marching in place along with the
returning troops in Aida, swaying and sobbing with the chorus of
slaves in Nabucco. But the well-prepared *New York Times* critics

Yawning as a profession

do not write to encourage this. All they do is slice off fragments of the
performance, technical fragments if possible, cutting them loose like
slivers of chicken gizzard, then hold them up to peer at, to sniff, and
finally to be flicked into a refuse box, labelled either 'unacceptable' or
perhaps 'quite nice'. It's like X-raying a pretty girl.

It is a cold life, necessary for advancement admittedly, necessary to take up those swirling opportunities that flow through the country and covered over the fissures which revealed the house-party of the very rich people, but still not a life anyone can take without some help. The reader has the past and future, great, but what is going to give him that sensation of the transistor radio popping on reassuringly inside him: where are his friends right here in the present?

There are several second-best consolations about. One is to just give up on people and try to make material things into his warm friends. With a lot of hi-tech devices, and especially the user-friendly computer, this is not too hard. On its surface that computer is a cold beast, used just to run spread-sheets, or access data banks. That seems nothing special. But yet, this device has been easily understood and liked, even by people who generally have little to do with mathematical creations. How could that be? Think again what that computer is. There's a hard exterior, made of metal and tough plastic and soldering welds and bolts. But yet within it, somehow invisible to the naked eye, somehow not even existent in any material way one can specify, there is the software, this ectoplasmic thing inside the hardware, which surges through the computer and makes the modem work and the lights flash and the screen flouresce up the words its user wants.

This is, of course, just what the human soul does for its owner. The reader emerges on his planet in the strange flesh-covered capsules he calls his body, it's made of squishy things and hard bits and there are hairy parts and, as its possessor knows only too well when he feels sluggish, when he does not at all want to go through the grind of heading out to work, but rather would be happy to stay dawdling at the breakfast table all day, by itself this odd container would just sort of shlump down and not do anything at all. Only his inner soul can do anything to energize it and make him a proper, efficient, advancing being. That's why in putting his disks in the computer in the office later and watching it light up he will be recognizing a kindred soul. With his disks and instructions and the immediacy of the user-friendly handle he will actually be reaching across the interpersonal void to make a link from what's inside him, to the thing that's almost a soul inside it.

But there is a better consolation, and one tucked away, right at the center of the *New York Times*, in the last place the non-initiated would expect. This is the column of James Reston – the most respected commentator in America, the man who covers hard

politics, what would seem the most butch, tough subject one can
imagine. But yet, when he does it, there is a glimpse of something
other than coldness, harshness, distant power:

> **The President is back at the White House, to everyone's
> relief, but his aides are still sore at the press . . .**
>   (July 21, 1985, shortly after Reagan's cancer operation)

> **The question for President Reagan and General Secretary
> Gorbachev is . . . merely whether they can knock off the
> propaganda for a while . . .**
>   (column shortly before the 1985 summit)

There is a cozy comfy softness in this. To keep it from being too
obvious there is that trapping of public knowledge, all formal,
external, descriptive ('The President is back at the White House';
'President Reagan and General Secretary Gorbachev'); but inside
that, and it comes up in all Reston's writing, there is also private
knowledge, informal good guy talk, the sort of thing we say among
friends ('but his aides are still sore'; 'knock off the propaganda for a
while').

After that softening up, after giving this hint that the reader is not
excluded from the subjects of his columns, Reston tucks his legs up
and dives down, down, down into the inner motivations, the core
feelings of these powerful men:

> **President Kennedy failed at his 1961 summit meeting
> with Nikita Khrushchev in Vienna partly because he paid
> too much attention to detail and tried to go it alone. He
> had been told that President Eisenhower did not impress
> the Soviet leaders at the summit because he always turned
> to Secretary of State John Foster Dulles for answers.**
>   (pre-summit column)

But of course! The readers have all wanted to impress someone in a
meeting. They all know that terrible feeling of overcompensating
when they're nervous. They could, if they wanted, it seems, now
hover in the doorway of the Cabinet room and yell out a statement of
what the men in there are feeling and it would be so accurate, so
precise that they would twist around startled in their places at the oak
desk there, to see this mind-reader, this secret sharer of all that they

hold. These men, through Reston, are made his friends. That's the trick. It is just what the tabloids tried. Since the politicians stand for all America, then indirectly the readers are hooked up with all America – with the ultra-rich and other *Times* readers and tabloid readers and even those welfare mothers and St. Raphael emblazened criminals we came in on – through them.

It's a tempting promise, straight out of Augustine's City of God, for it suggests that friendship is the way to turn this squabbling earth into a sharing heaven after all. It's not perfect, not as good as a feeling of real direct contact with others would be. Also it's not true: the people on top are not really that similar, have many other interests and controllers of their action. But it will have to do.

5

New York Times II: Mozart and Bruce

If there is one music festival that is genuinely popular among *New York Times* readers, one that they go to by inner prompting, spontaneously, without duress, it is the 'Mostly Mozart' series at Lincoln Center every summer. There it would be very rare for them to find sitting in the next seat a confirmed reader of one of the down-market papers. If in the darkened hall they did see him, a man who had wandered into Lincoln Center thinking it might be an advanced booking office for the next Knicks basketball game perhaps, they would see an individual in torment. He would fidget, he would be bored, he would look at the ceiling or play with the plush covering on the back of the seat in front of him or fold and unfold his Knicks souvenir roster card: anything but listen to that *awful* stuff coming from the orchestra. Okay, there might be occasional good tunes, something a guy could hum along with, but there's only a bit of that, you have to wait *ages* for a good tune dropped in to come back, to be repeated in its original form, to give you something to grab on to after all that screechy stuff in between. Even then they cheat you on the repeated tune, the musicians on stage insist on playing it strangely when they reach it the second or third time, it's all distorted, different.

The outcome is clear. There will be more crumpling and uncrumpling of the Knicks roster card; more fidgeting and grimacing and exasperated clicking and grunting; enough perhaps till the other people, the regular attenders, look furiously over and grunt back; and then the misplaced unhappy one is free, there is no longer even the appearance of decency to keep up, he can leave, flee, escape; race down the crazy twisting stairwell, suffering further indignities of electrostatic shock from the metal bannister, but that doesn't matter, he's almost out, to the doors, the street, the concrete and the real city. Let those hoity bums left inside suffer that garbage.

Which they do gladly. They love the tunes, they savor their distorted reappearance; and as to those long boring bits in between: they are exquisite. It is, of course, the *New York Times* reader's life.

79

What is Mozart but the particular series of transformations they know so well? It is not pure transformation, arbitrary at the start and arbitrary to the end: that would be unpleasant, and also hard to get a grasp on. Mozart's transformations are much more controlled. They start off with something graspable, that tune our die-hard Knicks supporter had as his sole relief. Then, most important, the transformations that do come are always presented in an interlinked, interdependent series: always through dominant, always back to tonic. This makes their underlying logic a match to the carefully assessing, carefully examining and considering attitudes the *New York Times* readers have come to depend on in mapping out their professional careers. Even the transitional bits in Mozart are exciting, in tension, because there are a tremendous number of possible ways they might develop, but these alternate future states, though they would be dependent on a part of the transformation that came earlier, have not, cannot, yet have been decided upon. In the first movement of the symphony when will the second tune switch back to the home key? It's going to get back, we know it, we're sure, but how exactly? When will the composer choose to strike? This is thrilling. This is fun. This is the examination of that terrain of alternate futures we started with, and at that most thrilling moment when the choice of intervention is about to be made.

New York Times readers get to see a warily transforming life lived out in Mozart; they also get a reminder that it's a delightful life, that assessing, studying alternate futures, and weaving interdependent logic into the past and future, is not just a possible thing to do but a *good* thing, a recommended thing, to do. Is not the future confident, rosy, ready for action, when you stride out of Lincoln Center 11 pm the concert over? The process of your life has been there, on display, and it works. It was in the main development of the piece, and also in the incidentals. Along the way, as all the switching and selecting and to-ing and fro-ing was going on, orchestra banging and audience hooked, Mozart provided comfortable way-stations of graspable tunes. That is encouragement. You will transform – for those tunes are distorted variants of the original ones – yet there is no fear that the various intermediate states you will have to work yourself into along the way will be scary ones – for those way-station tunes in Mozart are beautiful indeed. If there are unpleasantnesses, clashing chromatics or minor ninths, they're soon overcome with more sweetness, more triads and other reassertions of stability and even bliss. Who could resist going ahead when that path is sure to be so sweet? Even someone who worries whether the person they're turned into at the very end will be all right is provided for. At the end of a Mozart symphony there will be a coda: a strong and satisfying arrangement of notes, different from the very first one perhaps, but not too different, since it's back in that stable and pleasantly recognizable home key. Even if you follow the transformation all the way, it says, you will be in a good state at the end. The concept of a judicious, though still limited, self-transformation of man, is deep in Mozart's music, as it was in reformist Masonic circles in late eighteenth-century Austria. That is what the Lincoln Center audiences throng for. There is much classical music they sit through only because of its social cachet. But Mozart they genuinely want.

Would it be possible to have a music that matched, not the *New York Times* world, but the simple 'making everything constant and familiar' attitude of the tabloids? It couldn't be a symphony or concerto or any other complex form – all those have too much internal development and change. Regular key changes would have to be minimized too – for the if-then possibilities must not be left to tempt, the tensions of changes to another tune or key must not be left open. All there could be space for would be one item, brought like a lassoed horse into a corral, which would there have done to it the only thing that can happen in that stockade of the continuous present: it would be repeated: regularly, monotonously – but indispensable for this style of thought to work.

It does not sound enticing, conductive to interest or delight, but apparently quite a few people think otherwise, for this is the recipe for almost every popular hit song of the past fifty years. A tune is stated, then repeated; a slightly different tune is stated, and then the first one is repeated. It is done on simple and instantly recognizable subjects – the famous searching, finding or losing of love; and it is done using the most familiar chords of the Western sound system, that too being the most familar thing imaginable when it comes to transposing a style of thought into sound.

The technique is stripped to its simplest in what was perhaps the most popular song in America this decade: Bruce Springsteen's 'Born in the USA'. This is a tune that includes a certain amount of repetition. The author informs us where he was born, and then, in case the information imparted might have been unclear, repeats that statement thirteen times in the rest of the song. One can detect a certain chauvinism in the chorus – those not born in the American continent south of Canada and north of Mexico are beyond consideration, and disfavored from birth – which also would not have made it difficult to grasp in the then Reagan-voting America. The notes form but a short melodic fragment, and, to reduce needed attentiveness, the verse and chorus are carried on the same tune. All possible variation is suppressed. The tune is straight *forte*. The color of the spoken voice dominates the musical voice – i.e. it is barely snug. There is no rise and fall, no shape, no change of key, no development, and, especially, no reason for the song to end where it does. The artist could go on shouting indefinitely. It is like a towering public housing project, which once the pattern for one floor has been made can be repeated for twenty stories, or perhaps for forty stories: it makes no difference. There is nothing new anywhere along. It is life in the present-tense stockade. The only tension, the only hint of time in the song, is that eager moment when the listener expects the verse to return to the title chorus, which he knows will be coming up, just as before, totally unchanged, any moment now – so long as he just waits.

Through the recurring tune, through the ever-constant, ever-repeating present, the world is being turned from a threat into something comfortable. Even words that you might think would bring in the past or the future are, through the chanted repetition, made meaningless, and just left as sounds in the present. When a Liverpool crowd yells "Here we GO!", or a rock audience calls out 'BORN! in the U–S–A', they are not making an effective move to escape the bounds of the present, even though the words are ostensibly about progress or birth. This is a good thing, because while eternity and rebirth are useful concerns for the Lincoln Center audience, objects they can work with, they would be discomfiting, a reminder of weakness and insignificance, for the type of Mr Springsteen's fans to dwell on at length. Yet through a coarsened, tuneless yelled chorus, they can be made safe. His listeners are no longer worried by life or eternity when Springsteen is done. Rather they are in the stockade where they know they belong. Variability, alternate futures, and second-guessing are dropped without worry. There is a little populist kvetching in the words against those in the outside world who have pushed the listeners into this stockade, but it's not enough to get anyone riled up.

In a gentler era an occasional popular song could add meaning to a word, as did 'Yesterday', with its regretful, haunting tune that enhanced the concept of that lost day before now. But that is rare. Even the endings to popular commerical songs are not stirring codas, but usually just a gentle repeat and fade, the sound engineer pressing steadily down, down, down on his volume levers – producing the perfect restatement of a present-tense stockade, floating along but having no power to surge out and act. If there is a loud chord at the end it will rarely be quite as the opening, but rather have added notes, or a broken phrase on top – all of which will again leave the listener hanging, caught in his continuous present, not ready for, not encouraged for, any decisive action out there.

The point is not that readers of the down-market papers are the only ones to listen to such music. Other factors contribute too. Rather it's that this sort of music is what the tabloid attitude turns into when compressed into three to five minutes and dumped on to the Western tonal system. The useful conclusion is the reverse one. There are some people who listen to this extraordinarily limited music desperately, repeatedly, exclusively – and they are likely to come from groups where that attitude of reassurance via the familiar runs strong. It is not all a bad thing: there can be a tremendous comfort in such simple, present-reasserting, tones. The attitude might be permanent, as with many readers of the down-market papers, or it might be temporary, as with the young of those better dressed citizens at Lincoln Center, who until they get their marching orders after university will be on the receiving end of an apparently unchangeable life too. But if that's what they think, that's the music they will seek.

6

New York Times III:
The American Executive

Where do our explorations leave the original question of keeping order in America? The *New York Times* Business pages will reveal all . . .

In the beginning there is the blob. It is out there, somewhere, and it is growing and straining and threatening to burst in here any moment. We can tell it's out there, because almost everything in the business pages is suffering its effects. Everything is surging and jolting upwards, or fading and faltering downwards. This is not just the stock market, with its mysterious bouts of health or tiredness; it is also, as almost any sample business section will show, something that occurs in the areas of housing ('A resurgence in the housing industry is visible here'), in movie theatres ('the price of a ticket had jumped . . .', 'Mr Alterman expects the number of screens to jump . . .'), in computers ('the profits of computer firms slumped'), and even in those chinless plastic delights, the Cabbage Patch dolls ('. . . it bounces back;' 'profits nearly quintupled . . .') (examples from business pages, *New York Times*, July 21 and 22, 1985).

Why are there all these surges and sags? This is unclear. At heart it is the people who are responsible, surging this way and that, but why they do it, and when exactly they're going to switch their impulses and start surging another way; that no one can tell. It is mysterious. All the business page can do – all the American vision of the blob at home can do – is somehow put these surges under sensible control.

For that the corporation is needed. It is a curious concept – the thirteenth-century canon lawyers who came up with the notion never could puzzle out whether corporations could be excommunicated – but on the *New York Times* business page it is accepted as the natural and only thing that can stand over, guide and control the blob. The imagery is much like riding a bronco. When the blob storms out and kicks, the corporation on top begins to bounce. Not only is there a housing boom, but a vice-president of the Boston-based C.W.C Builders Inc. says (July 22) that 'We're going crazy' trying to keep up with it; not only is there a jump in movie attendance, but a vice-president of the National Association of Theater Owners says (July 22) that his companies 'are building like mad' trying to keep up with that too. The effort is precarious, but exciting. If the corporation is skilful it stays on – and as an added treat the rollicking bulge-eyed and saliva-foaming bronco-blob it has wrapped its legs around is kept from getting loose and marauding in the stands.

What's going on is the domination of selling over buying. There is a great psychological difference. When you buy something you might receive pleasure in exchange for those plastic cards or pieces of paper you hand over, but when you sell something you receive power. The corporation, by building those theaters, constructing those houses, is selling to the masses. It is not responding, but controlling. Selling is like being a judge up on a grand chair above the witness: you can scowl, snigger, smile or be gentle, but he is in your hands, your control. You ask the questions, and give him only a limited range of answers. So long as you are quick, keep an eye on the witness and his moves, and above all keep those questions – those sale-offerings – coming in there like a knife, you can't lose.

This is why corporations are good if they're lean. Leanness is a positive term that apparently cannot be overused:

> **In addition, Merrill Lynch offers a new report, The Reshaping of American Industry, focusing on 29 companies currently being restructed for leaner, more efficient, more competitive operation.**
> (Merrill Lynch advertisement, July 23, 1985, p. 10 of the business section)

> **[The Comcast Corporation] is considered among the best-run companies in the industry . . .**
> **'Comcast, like Capital Cities, brings a lean management style to the table,' said Barbara Dalton Russell, an analyst at Prudential-Bache Securities.**
> (July 23, 1985, top story p. 1 of the business section)

Being lean means that you're the opposite of that blob you spend so much time closely straddling. If you weren't lean you might be mistaken for it. Worse still, you might even be taken over by it: becoming one with the blob and its raw certain-to-decay corporeal essence, instead of remaining appart, pure, in the clearer realm of spirit. This is especially important in the US, where there is such displeasure when an average constituent of the mass, an average person flashed on the TV screens for those moments of man-on-the-street reaction interviews, is bulgingly, quiveringly, swelling-out-the-doubleknit-floral-pantsuitingly, fat.

Blob-aversion will even sometimes extend from corporate structure to novitiates within those structures. Stroll through lower Manhattan at lunch hour and you'll see groups of immaculately suited senior businessmen hurrying along with a few younger ones – clones almost – scurrying along behind. But these are clones with a difference. For although the senior businessmen are usually of ordinary weight, the younger ones – fresh from Yale and Stanford, immaculately suited too – are often slender, thin and skinny. It seems more than just the physiology of trim youth; it seems almost a choice, a sign, an attempt by the youngsters to carry the whole corporation around in their oh-so-lean bodies; a frantic demonstration that even though their jobs don't yet show it they *can* be as agile, non-blobby, and quickly responsive as the whole corporation must.

The reason blobs are recognized as growing fat and ponderous is that they are, of course, just the physical form of our old 'pulling-everything-into-the-familiar' popular attitude. Let everything pile in, nothing come out, and a dangerously swollen behemoth form is the result. Who knows what it might do? The background fears and energy on the business page are the same as our fears of what the non-thoughtful masses around us can potentially do. Through those entities called corporations the careful assessment attitudes of the proper middle-class *New York Times* reader are being turned to face the dangers of his brethren in the nation. It is especially complicated because in America the masses are not just the workers – what made a fine and quite sufficient enemy for Pasteur and traditional European reactionaries – but anyone who is not right now sharing our particular assessment worries. Somebody who is worrying and assessing, but worrying about and assessing different things, will, by his distance, become another item in the vast population mass we are immersed in.

The problem, once again, is that of assuring mass-coherence in America, without degenerating into the simple mass of the blob. To have a corporation controlling the mass is a good start, but to see the real solution we need to go further, and consider the executive who

controls the big corporation, the head honcho, the hero, big macher
and king.

Who is he? At one time it would have been easy to say. He was the
opposite of the artist. The artist was long-haired, concerned with
emotions, and lived a life of such profligacy, such lack of concern for
money or money's decay, that he would frequently be reduced to
poverty and – worst! – not even be worried about it. This was the
opposite of the late Victorian businessman, and as it became
developed into a fine art (the artistic persona, if not so frequently the
production) it was easy to read back the characteristics of the
individual it was designed to oppose. The businessman would be
conventionally dressed, concerned with material objects, and do
anything, from double-entry bookkeeping to loan rate calculations,
to keep the possibility of future money loss away. Also, most
importantly, he would do it by himself: taking his thoughts into a
private realm, non-observable and incomprehensible to the outsider
realm, where he would figure out deals, scheme takeovers, and
generally create the magic that would make him large, great, and
monetarily strong. It was the sort of thing that the most popular
literature heroes from this era of the robber barons did: Tarzan and
Holmes also would retreat into a special not properly observable
realm (African jungle, London low-life) from which they would
draw nourishment and re-emerge, back in society, with a power that
no one else had.

Today of course that individual magic is largely gone. Artists in the
New York Times do not go to Paris, grow their hair long, give no
thought for the morrow, or let the private muse strike. They attend
interactive creativity maintenance seminars, video retraining centers,
and, in the case of one lucky Los Angeles television writer ('Plays
Blossom at the O'Neill Center', July 21, 1985, p. 47), get to
appropriate time for the O'Neill Theater Center National Playwrights Conference (associated with the Center for the National
Opera/Music Theater Conference), which is funded by Exxon and
other companies, and is the ideal place for the bureaucratized creative
juices to flow. Only on the sports page do Americans allow
individuals of exceptional, mysteriously-granted abilities to exist.
There such powers are safe because they are locked in the clearly
limited bounds of what is but a game. You can only hit so many home
runs a year in baseball, and even if you do hit more than Hank Aron,
you are still limited to the sub-world of baseball. In business there are
no such natural bounds. An excecutive with magical powers could

grow indefinitely. As he's there to run the corporation that's holding down the already infinitely-straining blob, this would not be a fruitful strategy. What we need is a strong business head, but one without the possibility of infinite and so scary growth. Yet how else can we give him strength if he's not allowed to have too much power himself?

The answer is method. It works in silly subjects:

> **'It's not the toy business today,' Mr. Greenberg said (discussing his company's Cabbage Patch doll sales). It's the entertainment business. We no longer invent single hot products. We invent an umbrella concept, a whole family of products.'**
> ('Coleco Moves out of the Cabbage Patch', July 21, 1985, p. F4)

And it works in serious subjects:

> **Merrill Lynch & Company, the corporate parent of the nation's largest securities firm, announced yesterday that Daniel P. Tully had been elected president and chief operating officer . . . 'When I became chief executive last July,' Mr Schrever [the previous head of the company] said, 'it was during the beginning of a structural cost control program that I wanted to implement myself. Then I had two months off for bypass surgery, and when I came back and assessed who did good work and who I could count on, I saw it was Dan Tully.'**
> ('President is Elected at Merrill Lynch', July 23, 1985, p. D2)

Dan Tully runs Merrill Lynch & Company because Dan Tully knows how to play ball. With method the problems of genius and unfettered growth are gone. All is averaged out, restrained and smoothed. Flukes, individualism, and arbitrary and unpredictable changes are gone. Here at the peak, at the very top of the corporation, on the penthouse floor, in the highest executive suite, the *New York Times* takes us across the plush carpet and right on into the Chief Executive Officer's brain, there to reveal a realm of pure order, clarity, restraint, and law. That is the secret, the solution, the cure.

It is the opposite of the blob, and has several pleasant consequences. Being method rather than intuition, it is open to all. Your intuition or genius is something that goes on mysteriously within your brain, and from which I am barred; but your method, your sure-fire procedures and rules, that is something I and everyone else can in theory come up close to and take a good peer at. It is the world of public, investigable rationality, which is being carried out at the top of our corporations. All is on view, in theory if not always in fact. It is the consolation of publicity: what Louis XIV was doing when he had his nobles schlep into the toilet with him; what that Los Angeles writer at the O'Neill Theater Center National Playwrights Conference pouring out her writing had to go through, since:

> **. . . almost all activities at the center are open for observation . . . there are visits from national delegations (a Chinese contingent visited last week), from representatives of regional theaters, executives of commercial theaters, members of arts boards, and financing personnel.**
> ('Plays Blossom at the O'Neill Center', July 21 1985,
> p. 47)

When the technique is available to all, no one, no ordinary person's contribution, can feel left out. Cynics might suggest that some of the corporations described so neatly on the *New York Times* business page depend on closed markets, unjust taxes, bribes disguised as commissions or consultancies, and other nefarious doings, and that entrepreneurs would fail if they tried to get ahead by following the rules it shows. But the features on the *New York Times* business pages are not there for cynics. They are for believers, or those who would be believers. Who wants to know about nefarious doings? It's much more fun to learn about ideals. What the business pages do accordingly is show the friendly sharing standards of Augustine's heavenly city being used to build up corporations, those powerful entitities which are at the heart of our hard and factual earthly life. Corporations might seem big, and strong, but now they they are not *too* big and strong, not too scary and separate from us. Instead they are of us, since they contain the possibility of our comprehending them.

What's happening is a return to the people. The Corporation controls the blob, the Executive controls the corporations, and on the very top of it all, controlling the executive, is . . . the People themselves. It is a return full circle, in a wonderful self-maintaining solution. By worshipping and respecting their corporations, Americans are worshipping and respecting themselves. They are what direct the all-important corporate method, what give force, direction and energy to it. Otherwise the method could become a stodgy, old-fashioned, set-in-its-way sort of thing, and while that might be good enough for Prussia or Ruritania, it is not good enough for Americans.

Sometimes the self-worship that the market shows takes a transparent extreme. These are all those goods that represent exactly what The People are: clothes and furniture and car styles and even . . .

> **Mr. Greenberg [company president] speaking:**
> **'. . . Cabbage kid [dolls] are all different. They are not perfect. They represent you and me with all our warts.'**
> (Coleco Moves out of the Cabbage Patch)

To transform people into Cabbage Patch kids which the corporations can then offer, is an effective way of taming the population indeed. Any fad will do, if it's popular enough, because such fads are nothing but the concentrated image of the people who support it.

Even in less direct ways the blob as transmuted and simplified through the market will work itself into a form that the executive trying to energize and direct his corporate method can deal with. The people lose their raw, potentially scary power, because they have been grouped into this understandable and abstract form of preferences in the market. And the executive, wielding his corporation to match that market, is also freed of potentially scary individual power, because the economic forces, being necessary, must be followed. Magic is driven out from top and below: executive and blob are contained, because each feeds off the order of the other that arises when wishes and the response to wishes are carried out.

There is a certain historical precedent for this. The market of Friedmanite and conservative fame is a prayer session, which puts priest and parishoner at ease. It is no evangelical shriek, but a stately High Church or non-comformist ritual – just as Adam Smith (who with most advanced thinkers of his time was strongly against zeal in religion) would have found right. The parishoner merely needs to accept that he be sensitive to the wishes of his flock, and that way everyone in the church will be pleased:

> **You have to talk to buyers and customer and find
> out what's hot and what isn't, [Mr. Greenberg]
> said. 'And you have to understand the culture of
> our society. Looking at the success of 'Rambo'
> and seeing the application to military toys. Look-
> ing at the cult of Madonna. Even understanding
> this Coke thing and seeing if it has any lessons
> . . .'**
> (Coleco Moves out of the Cabbage Patch)

There is no problem with ethics, or priorities, or any other aspect
of will except that of what people want. In that specific realm the
approach is superb: nothing is too small, too insignificant or hidden to
be overlooked. The market will see everywhere, as God once did
before it. And with the omniscience of both, there is the same
comfort in both. The apparatus speaks to you and you alone, because
it responds to any wish you have. It is that pleasure of hooking up to
user-friendly computers again.

Smith and the other eighteenth-century codifiers of modern
political economy were explicit on this religious substitution. About
his system of a market, which goes into natural equilibirum through
prices, Smith wrote:

> **The sovereign is completely discharged from a
> duty, in the attempting to perform which he must
> always be exposed to innumerable delusions, and
> for the proper performance of which no human
> wisdom or knowledge could ever be sufficient.'**
> (Wealth of Nations, Modern Library edition, 1937,
> p. 651)

The task is beyond human comprehension, and so it will be a Godly
thing that produces the answer. With Smith it is no longer God
himself, but the people, and specifically they as what he called 'private
people' in social dealings with each other, with the individual choices
they make about what trades to take and how hard to work or
innovate in them. This is the finding of God in the doings of the Social
World, which is where an optimist would hope to find Him whether
heaven has fallen on to earth or not.

That's what makes sense of the Invisible Hand. Since the USA is an
intensely religious country, the beneficient linking structure of such a

ghostly yet powerfully grasping thing will be ready to be believed in by very many there. Indeed, one reason for the USA being so religious is perhaps the fact that many people living in it have experienced over a generation or two a non-humanly directed but all-encompassing background thing (what they are told is the national free market) which did increase their happiness and wealth. The persuasion is that of belief through the proof of material success – another approach with a certain, generally self-pleasing, religious precedent.

To outsiders it might seem coarse when strong religious believers link general necessity and business necessity or use them so similarly, but that is just because outsiders haven't experienced the joy of this double deontological oomph. Think how useful and simplifying it must be to be able to justify what you do by saying it is God's will. You always know how to act, and you can always justify trying to get your way, because God has told you so. With a strong enough belief in the market, justification by reference to Business can be just as strong. 'I'd like to give you the money but, heck, you know, business is business.' Both God and Business simplify life, and are useful in letting you carry out your intentions. People are not being impious when they use the two together. They are just, in both cases, getting the delight of sliding along the same encompassing background structure of necessity.

Since the market replaces or substitutes for God, it must also offer the sort of consolation about death that we expect any good religion to give. This it does. When the American executive needs a criterion to energize his method, the one he will invariably take is the one that will bring him fastest into the future. It might be management techniques, or computer control systems, or particular hi-tech items of production, but in every case it's the freshest and latest mankind can achieve. The reasoning is curious, but persuasive. In 1988 almost everyone has a color television. In 1960 hardly anyone had one, but the few who did were touching something special. They were actually merging, quite closely, with something that would be active and widespread twenty-eight years later. The more of themselves they gave to worship and appreciation of the spanking new device of the color television back there in 1960, the more of themselves would be bridging the gap to the living future that would be sure to come. It is the way that for people of different table manners from our own, ingesting a warrior's heart will guarantee valor for the eater. The more you chew those ventricles – the more vigorously you love the new – the more your personal survival is being guaranteed.

In a different form this reasoning is familiar to us all. It is the traditional consolation of secular intellectuals, that by producing great works they will not face complete oblivion, because these remnants of themselves will survive after their deaths into the future. The weak point in this traditional consolation is that the intellectuals or artists can't guarantee that their works will survive. (Which is why they agonize so much. If they don't produce good enough work they are not merely disappointed, but doomed.) The standard American solution is better, because you do not need to produce any great artifact at all for it to work. The remnants already exist: they are the new items or ways of living that we are sure will occur in the future. It is not a matter of trust. There is proof. Our hi-tech items are instances where the future has become sloppy, and let part of itself slip back a bit, into the present where we now live. Grabbing on to those items or techniques, we are grabbing dangling ropes from the great beyond. All we have to do is hold tight, and they will pull us forward with them. This might be called the Tarzan theory of individual survival.

A certain selective attention is necessary for it to work – you can't pay too much attention to all the items that immediately become old-tech and are thrown away when the new stuff comes in – but that is not hard. It is what happens whenever a new hit makes it to the Top 20 record charts. The new arrival means that an old one has to leave, yet few people say: 'Dig that hot new hit on the Top 20 chart! How it makes me reflect on the inevitable decay of man and all his endeavors.' Such mourning is rare. The attention is on the new, the one that has just slipped down into our presence from the future. That's the one we want to be.

This solution contrasts with what might be called the Time Capsule theory of immortality, more popular in Europe, where one respects the past and the past's set forms which are hoped to reproduce unchanged in the future, with the believer or perhaps his progeny sealed up along in them. Both theories have the advantage of letting you survive without having to bother about producing much of anything, and both also allow you to do so by copying the social forms of some group that's either already there or roughly outlined. Yet each pulls hard to make its surrounding country work in a certain way. The Time Capsule solution becomes a strong reason for the class system to go on: each class or sub-class will be a capsule to hunker down in, and will also provide most welcoming detailed rules of action. Plus, since the class system is a straight hierarchy, individuals at any one level will accept the existence of all the others, for otherwise the capsule they are in would break loose, drift off, and so no longer be guaranteed of getting carried on into the future. (This is not the only way European and especially British people think, of course, but is perhaps dominant, as evidenced by the way reformist moves have always had to push against this as something of a resilient core idea.) All this makes for a deep mutual miscomprehension with Americans, who would naturally downgrade the past and accept the future, even if they only get vague hints of what it is. To European eyes that produces a personality with a certain tension, earnestness, and apparently naive acceptance of what is to come, free of standards of comparison with the past. Tolerance has been known to be strained.

Once again for Americans it is the Social world creating the Political: the people's wishes seeming to energize the rules for the corporations that control them. Salvation through those dangling strands from the future becomes perhaps the deepest reason the *New York Times* refuses to describe all of what actually happens in business on the feature parts of their financial pages. (There are specialist hard business news items, but unlike the editorial page where Reston is our interpreter, here there are no conduits between those and the business features.) All we get instead are executives making sure that their corporations are new and improved, and so bringing the future every day closer to us. Accounts of stagnation, or new items that are but variants on the old – let alone systematic suppression of the new – are kept down. Such lackings are usually only mentioned in the *New York Times* if they are about to be made good. What we get is an insistence that the executives and their firms are only responding to trends – which is yet another guarantee that the future being sighted and brought back will be one that the mass of the people will fit right in to. Thus those surges of interest in new personalities or products, which occur with no sense of embarrassment, since in those surges the nation is managing to love itself and the new together.

Each national solution to mortality is a distortion, but is, of course, partially true, and through repetition can be made to be felt as even more thoroughly true. For America, the consequences are abundant. Visiting Europe becomes pleasant, for since it's thought that the natives see America as their future, then the visitors can feel like returning Gods. The Soviet Union, apparently violating the American solution to the salvation problem by having a different vision of the future dangling out there to reach, becomes an abomination. Hi-tech military equipment becomes admired in itself, because it is the clearest possible sign of the new and the future. Planes are excellent, because they literally take off and go Up There, and the Space Shuttle, that super-plane, is even better:

> **The Challenger crew was pulling us into the future, and we'll continue to follow them.**
> (From Reagan's televised speech, January 28, 1986, the day the Shuttle exploded shortly after take-off)

Corporate interests in these devices are secondary, almost invisible. That is why dissent from Reagan's Star Wars plans has to concentrate on aspects such as whether it will work or how it will affect university research, rather than the source point of how the aerospace firms encouraged the government to back it because of the great scoops of money they would get. It would be disturbing, wrong, to dwell on that – because corporate interest is the only possible way one can imagine the great glob of people in America being organized.

Which leads to the final, and most distinctive, consequence. Through the mix of Tarzan salvation, and businesses ostensibly created out of the people, America gets a harmony that is not stagnant. This is an immensely powerful state of being, which has only rarely been achieved in history. All the Americans surging on the streets, hustling about their business, miraculously manage to do their surges and hustling in harmony. For they are all sure that they're going to the same place – and they can't wait.

Part Three
Some History

Where did the background ideas we've been considering so far come from — the nervous yet advancing life of the New York Times *type, the rule-following blue-collar workers; even those notions of salvation and the Other Side and now personal ambition we're all so concerned with? A look at money — which people have cared about greatly, and recorded their dealings with over a very long time — is a good way to bring out some answers, and show what it feels like to live in our money-suffused world today.*

7
Money and Personality

I.   Sky was good and Sky was hot and Sky was also, as his friends hunched eager in a semi-circle around the crap shoot, ready for him to let loose the dice in his hand, convinced that it was time to sing. In a 2/2 beat, starting on A flat, he let it pour out:

Luck be a lady twooo-night!
Luck if you've ever
   been a lady to begin with,
Luck! be a lady two-niiiiiight!!!

He sang it again and his friends joined in, sweeping their thick wads of used five-dollar bills in front of them as they strained for the low notes; he sang it once more, alternating with their chorus, and he even started to sing it another time, this time twisting his body ready for the dramatic leap-slide-skid that would see him actually unleash the dice, when the assistant director yelled:

'Cut it! What's with the song?! It's too soon!'

All action froze, and for a brief second, before the lights went out, the tableau on the sound stage was lit like a dream. There was Sky Masterson and his cronies – Nathan and Rusty Charley and big Nicely-Nicely – all hunched together tight, a small and brilliantly spotlit world of human-ness and shared intensity; and there was also, out beyond them, where the beam of the single 2,000 watt overhead arc light died away, a pool of darkness, first limpid and inky at the edge of the beam, but then utterly black, dark and empty, stretching away on all sides, reaching apparently without end to infinity.

What Sky and his friends were doing on the sound stage is a good image for one basic type of human dealing. It's what happens when you go down to the garage with a wad of used fives and ask the attendant to fix something for you, just you and he, no need to fill in forms or let anyone else know about it. It's also what happens when you buy a newspaper from a stand, pick up a second-hand car for cash, pay at a bar. There's no signing or invoices; no contacting the larger outside world to let Them know what you have done. That's

99

why there's such a feeling of complicity in these dealings. It is just you and the person you're paying, in a personal bubble, encased in your choice of face-to-face dealing, but otherwise all alone, two spotlit creatures on an otherwise empty stage.

The contrast with paying by credit card is total. There the payment seems personal – there is the flourishing signature you get to put on the receipt, the personal and attentive smile you get from the girl at the airport car reservation, the waiter hovering just for you at the expense-account restaurant – but in fact it is nothing of the sort. The deal is not pesonal or private or restricted to you two at all. Nathan, Rusty and Nicely-Nicely would skeedaddle if Sky Masterson said let's go on with the game but how about we all pay with our credit cards. His fences wouldn't want to know him. Even darling Adelaide would suspect something was up. Pay by credit card and everyone out there, the Authorities, the System – da Fuzz! – would have a way of finding out what was going on. They could trace back from the receipts and countersignings and indelible identification numbers, and follow them back, across the city and down the crawlways all the way to the hidden space under the city where the crap game was going on. There would be no privacy, no shared and secret complicity between Sky and the guys hunched close around him on the crap shoot. There would be a raid, the outside world bursting in, truncheons flying and police photographer flash bulbs popping and, well, the end of that community where Sky's friends could sing and sway in time with him, waving their wadded bills, and hoping that Luck, acting alone, without intervention or support from the distant outside world, could get him where he wanted. As the single overhead spot pulls up we would see that the sound stage was not empty, not stretching black in the distance, but filled, loaded around the rim, with records departments and clearing houses and computers and attentive, steel-rimmed-eyeglass-wearing clerks; all glaring so bright, as the spot rises up catching their chrome and glass, all making so much noise, as they emerge from the dark and we see them fuss and clank and whir along, that the poor flashily dressed big spenders at the crap shoot are drowned out by light and sound, humiliated, made small, pinioned like struggling butterflies on the bullseye of a giant target.

In which world are we? A little bit of both, of course, but ever more of the latter, of the credit card and check world, where smiling rent-a-car hostesses turn around and input our particulars into the computer, where the waiter does a computer check on our credit card number on his way to the kitchen. Credit card and private check transactions now far surpass cash in all private payments by value. It is highest in America, but other countries – Britain, Germany – are coming on strong. What does this mean? The question is one of how the background forces around us come into our personal world. In the direct cash transactions we use the system to create a private bubble for us, holding all the rest away; in the credit card world we feel private but in fact the whole world, all of time and fate, collapses down on us, pinioning us in place. The difference is a vast and unclear one, yet somehow seems to be acted out, to depend on and reveal itself in those particular little items of money – that flurry of cash, those omnipresent credit cards – which we use within the different systems. They perhaps are the clue. They perhaps are little portholes to the Other Side, to the realm of cause and assumption that surrounds us; through them we could, by this blizzard of little items, each glinting with an image of the true forces behind them, even learn how the feelings of the Other Side gets transmitted on to us too.

The task is ambitious, and to make it easier, to find out how, if at all, money can generate and maintain meaning, it will be useful to look at some of the key historical steps in the development of our money. Only then can the consequences of that innocuous credit card be worked out; only then can the curious concept of the individual that out society is now urging on us be readily understood. There might be some nice insights into the history of science along the way, too.

II.   We begin in ancient Greece. It was, as we have been taught, the land of Odysseus and Achilles, of far-sailing warriors and a new, very modern, concept of the individual:

> **[They] exist in the unbounded void, being entirely separate from each other; they differ in shape, size, position and arrangement; and they move through the void, overtaking each other and colliding. Sometimes they bounce off in random direction, at others – because they fit together . . . – they become interlocked and so remain in association.**

This fragment sounds like a description of the voyagings and adventures of a whole world of brave Odysseuses, but as it turns out it is one of the writings of Democritus describing, not people, but his new concept of something he called 'atoms'. This is very odd – that scientific constructs such as atoms should be like voyaging human beings – and it becomes even odder when one realizes that when Democritus was writing he also had around him new objects called 'coins' (for it was in ancient Greece that coins were first invented) which too were separate hard items that usually stayed apart but could combine to create something new. Something was going on to produce similarities between these three disparate things – individual humans, scientific theories such as atoms, and coins. This means we've found the right place if we want to learn more about money as part of the cement of a conceptual universe. But whatever could the links among our curious triad be?

The central fact about ancient Greece, the simple physical backing to all that was there, as it were, was the curious dispersal of the Greeks around the central and eastern Mediterranean in tiny and separated city-states, so that they existed, as Plato put it;

Living around the sea like ants and frogs around a pond.

The geography encouraged this, because there were many little inlets where people could land, but then behind the inlets the land got so rough, so quickly, that there was only enough space for a small amount of crops to be grown. The settlers, once landed, were stuck, and thrown on to their own resources. Each city-state was like a little peak, rising up from the sea, distinctive and alone.

Which was exactly what the first coins were like. It has often been considered a mystery why the early ones were blank on one side (it's not a technical problem, as you can just as easily put a die on the punch, which makes the back, as on the anvil, which makes the front) but that of course is a perfect model, an accurate image, of this feeling of a settlement rising distinctively from the sea, the top inhabited and complex, the bottom shapeless, extending into the abyss. Greek cities identified with their coins. Andros had long had the emblem of an amphora, and so an amphora went on their coins; Seriphos had used the frog as an identifying symbol, and that is what went on their coins too. It was repeated throughout the Greek world as the striking of coins spread, civic devices on them almost all, a different one representing each particular city, encapsulating the citizen's feelings about the special foundation myths that had created them or the Gods that looked over them (Oligarchies, monetary pride swelling out even unto pictures of the richest men sweeping everything else off the coins, were the sole exceptions). When a city was leaving an alliance it would print new coins without the symbols of that old alliance; when it was refusing to join an alliance it would resolutely continue to stamp coins with its old particular symbol, as Melos did, in defiance of the Athenians, with the grievous consequences we know from Thucydides.

Even when the coins came to have two formed sides, this symbolism of their being the actual city settlement in miniature continued. Sometimes it would be the land rising out of the sea: with the back being a creature from the sea, and the front showing a creature or emblem from the land, from the city itself, which naturally was higher up, rising from the back of the coin as the city itself rose from the sea. Thus the gorgeous Eretrian coins, with the back showing a cuttlefish, tentacles curled in motion, and the front a placid nose-scratching cow, which on the actual island (known for its cattle) looked down on the sea. Sometimes the symbolism would have the heavens rising above the land, as with the first two-sided Athenian coins, where the top side had the Goddess Athena herself, up there in the eternal realm overlooking the city, be it from Olympus or just from the air, and the bottom, basely material side, had an image of the owl, the Goddess's sacred bird here on earth. It was, in either case, a vertical movement, from sea to land, or from land to the heavens – the simple metallic coin quite literally the city settlement, perched on the edge of the Mediterranean, suspended between earth and heaven, in miniature.

But this proud separation of each city, carried out in their coins too, was only half of the basic setting of the Greeks. Precisely because the land around the settlements was so rough, so unable to provide the large hinterland needed by an advanced city, each settlement was forced to trade with and depend on the other settlements scattered around that great pond. It has been estimated that it could cost more to haul grain seventy-five miles on land than to ship it right across the Mediterranean. On the basis of this inter-city trade, the common heritage, the unity among the cities was enormous. There was the intermingling of traders, the use of goods from other cities, the Pan-hellenic games, the sharing of basic Gods, and everywhere the shared language, which proved a common origin and similarity, and which was what made all the other inhabitants of the world into 'barbarians' – the disparaging term for people who could not speak Greek, and were thought to make only vile 'bar-bar-bar' sounds.

Yet, Greeks being Greeks, humans being human, this intermingling was not complete. Trading was necessary, but it was often
against each city's will, often with quibbling and fussing and a great
deal of self-important protest:

> **Nowadays we often see in countries and cities dockyards
> and harbors very conveniently placed outside the city, but
> not too far off . . . Cities thus situated manifestly reap the
> benefit of intercourse with their ports; and any harm
> which is likely to accrue may be easily guarded against
> . . .**
>
> (Aristotle's Politics, 1327a32)

Greece as a whole was interlinked, but hesitantly so. That was the
key. There were the Pan-hellenic games, but they were for
competition and to show the superiority of one city against the other;
there were the shared basic Gods, but Xenophon reports the Spartans
waking up early in war-time to pray to the Gods before other Greeks
could get their word in; there were also hundreds of local cults, each
greatly important, and each of which showed up the visitors who
didn't know them as not quite as pious as one would like. And even
though the visiting traders or travellers did speak Greek, and so were
not quite so bad as the great unwashed of Barbariandom, they still
were not quite right, still aliens if not foreigners, and hardly ever
granted citizenship, even unto the second generation.

This was the reason it was agony trying to get a long-lasting
alliance among the Greek city-states – an insight school-children ever
since, trying to memorize those interminable lists of one short-lived
federation after another, have been quick to grasp. If the Greek city-
states had been totally separate everything would have been easy; if
they had merged in a once-and-for-all total link-up it would have
been simple too. But no, there was one partial alliance and another,
then the full alliance against Persia and then dissolution into more
leagues, and then the attempt for dominance by Athens in its own
league, and the attempted rebellions, and etc, a mess of fussing and
ever-changing alliances only ended when Philip of Macedon put the
whole gang into *his* league.

Coins accorded with this hesitantly interlinked aspect of the Greek
situation too. They would, as we've seen, be changed as a city went in
or out of an alliance. But even more basically, although they were
separate bits of metal, like the separate city-states themselves, they
were at the same time bits of metal that carried a widely understood

value and could be used in interchange with others. That is what coins as currency means. Otherwise you have just emblems, like the little flag tie-pins Nixon put on when he was being photographed. The new-fangled coins of the Greeks contained in their very nature of being an exchangeable currency the concept of a polity where each side was ever ready to take advantage of the other but still talking and accepting some harmony in the advantage-taking – an accurate matching for a world of sharp-haggling traders.

This was by no means the only possible way to be. Many early civilizations had not had bargaining relations – goods were exchanged in customary order, at what were thought to be eternally fixed rates – and even when they did there was the problem of how much you could expect people you didn't know well, expecially beyond the borders, to accept the standards necessary for such unclear exchange. There are numerous methods for transferring property, not all involving coin currency or even money. The eight-foot tall green men landing in my garden with spaceships and ray guns say they want to take my pet poodle away. Our relation is simple. I can be vaporized or I can give in. It's an easy choice; I ask if they want the beast gift-wrapped or just straight. If they have qualms about vaporizing me, though, perhaps because they detect in me a distant, if runty and mutated, relation, or because they think I have a monopoly on poodles and they'll want to come back; if they've come to get what they want by quibbling rather than brute assault, then we will need some mutually understandable money to carry the deal. After all, there's a lot to be said for poochie. I will say it. They will say I must be joking, that yapping cur, look at its gums, they're doing me a favor to take it off my hands. I will rejoin. Nobody will take up crowbars or ray guns. Eventually we will compromise.

Take away the fanciful bits and this was what was going on in ancient Greece, both in trading and more generally, in that basic setting of separate yet semi-dependent cities. The trading was with near brethren; the symbols on the coin, verifying it as currency, were understood in all the Greek cities. Coin currency was money which showed even more shared values than brute chunks of metal as money. This then will be our first conclusion: the curiously linked yet still autonomous coins naturally matched, came from and encoded, the curiously linked yet still autonomous city-states. How could the practice of minting coins, once it had been invented on the very Eastern edge of the Aegean, have spread so quickly around the whole Greek regions otherwise?

The second step is even easier: this is to show that the nature of the citizens within each city-state also matched the island-like setting in which they lived. Certainly a formal analogy did exist. There was lots of public arguing and discussion within each city-state and it was accepted that there should be such arguing, just as there was lots of quibbling between the different city-states, about trade or overall alliances, and it was accepted that they would quibble so within an overall consensus of unity. Sometimes the outer limits of the consensus would be broached and there would be civil or inter-city war, but this was considered a slip from what should be. The sort of arguing allowed and indeed encouraged within an individual polis is clear even in the early seventh-century BC reforms of Solon, which produced interlinked and clear laws, open to discussion for their proper working.

Was the analogy not just chance, but causal? There are reasons to think so. This sort of internal city politics, of an allowed and public haggling before coming to a conclusion, is just what both the traders of each city and also the political leaders used to dealing with the other cities would find a natural expression of what they were doing anyway. We take some of the conclusions for granted, but we're used to them. Putting political debate to an open vote, which would then be binding on all the participants, was not what the Pharaohs, the Assyrian Kings, or many other ancient rulers would have considered a sensible way to run a country. But to a trader it is perfectly natural: a binding vote is like settling a commercial deal. Both are agreements not to argue any more; to let the disposition of symbolically geared-down forces (money, votes) at the end of a bout of mutual persuasion determine the solution. That the forces were symbolically geared-down from brute attack only makes the necessary abstraction easier. It is not fiat, or domination, but truce.

With both, the decision you end up with necessarily contains a remnant, a memory, of the argument that went into creating it. This does not happen with fiats. Stalin proclaims that the policy is to have socialist realism in art, and that's that. If there are any objectors, he will have seen that you won't get to hear of them. It's when your leader announces that a new temple is going to be built on the sacred hill, it's expensive but the vote went 823 to 417 for, that you get a carry-over of the argument – a frozen image of the truce – in the decision. Such carry-over voting is exactly what specialists in monetary bargaining would think natural. Given my druthers I'd value dear poochie at more money than all the mines of Laurion could produce, but as it is I settle for three drachmae. That price becomes a permanent record book, revealing my intentions, the buyer's intentions, and the degree to which we each moderated our intentions before coming to an agreement we could then freeze and act upon. If prices are memories of bargaining, then why shouldn't political decisions be such gentle memories too?

Not only is this what a trader would suggest, but it also makes life easier for me and all the others within the polity. Reporting a vote means respecting the voters. Each member gets to be there in any statement of what the whole is doing. Proof of this is that in ancient Greece a distinctive particularization syntax was used whenever political plurals were tossed around: it was always 'The Abderans decided such and such', never 'Abdera has decided such and such'. Were I a concerned Abderan, I would appreciate the former. Almost every other culture used the latter.

This mimicking from level to level sounds odd, but it's one that people do all the time. Where else are you going to get ideas? Also it's a compliment. Think of a contemporary salesman driving back from Houston to Amarillo, samples of refinery-control software systems on the back seat, collar loosened and cigarette stains on his fingers; driving back perhaps in an all-night slog on the highway, so that only as he's arriving does Dawn with her finger-tips of rose touch the horizon. He doesn't want to think that his city's the pits and his life is a bore. It's nicer to feel that his city somehow contains, carries out, the essence of what it means to be a good Texan; it's even nicer to feel that it's his own life and values that are being acted out there. Put him in a toga on a wind-taut freighter sailing back to his home settlement in Sicily, unsold amphorae on the back deck, dawn just rising on his politically bustling city, and the same feeling, the same gloriful feeling of appropriateness with the world, would be nice to have come out too.

Because the mimicking from the whole island setting to the individual city was so well carried out by those individual traders and indeed all the powerful citizens who had to deal with the other city-states, it's fair to expect yet another layer of hierarchial mimicking, this one going even further down, closer in, between the Greek city and the mind of the individual citizens within it. Here again there is good reason to think it was a mimicking jump the Greeks found easy to make. The great tragedies, for example, often showed how the overall choices that the city had to make were acted out by warring forces in an individual's mind. What Antigone was perplexed about was what the whole city would have to be perplexed about, and the nature of her decision would be a good model for the nature of theirs. Indeed these dramas were often shown in the aphitheaters that on other days would be used for real political debates, with the audience in both cases often being the same. All those prideful comments by Greek thinkers that Hellas was special because it had both great individuals and a great political system made by those individuals – in the polis – shows that they moved naturally between the levels of the mind and the city, finding the attributes of one necessarily reproduced in the other. Not every group of people were able to do it:

> **Those who live in a cold climate and in Europe are full of spirit, but wanting in intelligence and skill; and therefore . . . have no political organization, and are incapable of ruling over others.**

(Aristotle's *Politics*, 1327b25)

What you needed was a better sort of individual, for a better sort of political life:

> **But the Hellenic race . . . is . . . high-spirited and also intelligent. Hence it continues free, and is the best-governed of any nation.**

That's where psyche and city, to Aristotle's satisfaction, do match.

With this way of identifying both coins and people with the curious island setting of the Greeks, we're ready to go on to the third step: to see how the Greeks' experience of money could possibly be important in generating their even more scientific or philosophical thoughts about the universe. We should have some confidence that we're on the right track, since the odd man out of the Greeks, Sparta, relatively land-locked in its great plain, had a rigid prohibition on coined money – and produced no philosophers or scientists at all. Any results will be a nice check of our general point about the importance of handling different sorts of physical money – and, as an added bonus, perhaps give fresh insight into some of those thoughts which have survived to surround us now.

Rationalism is generally considered the first and highest of the Greeks' contributions. What seems to be assumed here is the notion of a 'fair' reason – one that's defensible against counter-attack. This is, of course, the approach we've just seen as being duplicated on the several levels, with the result that the same word can make sense in such totally different activities as 'fair' price (trading), 'fair' justice (individual), and 'fair' argument (politics). What each bracketed activity shares is that the parties involved in doing them are not likely to give in to what their opponent offers without a good, if non-violent, fight back. Traders are a cynical and unromantic lot, and quick to come back with a counter-argument when their customer or partner or any other human being proposes something to them. Mathematically precise prices are what they will be willing to realize as true; anything else is assumed to be an attempt to pull a fast one on them. Usually it is.

Politics too demands counter-arguments, whenever it has become something more than mere government. 'Government' is any making of decisions that are supposed to affect lots of people. It is an easy and often delightful activity that has appealed to maniacs throughout the ages. It can be carried on entirely behind closed doors, where the closest you get to argument is a stabbing in the eunuch's chamber, and the dominant ethos is the purported one of the Kennedy clan, 'Don't get mad, get even'. What distinguishes politics from this simple power-dealing is that it is government carried on at least partially in public, where it's accepted that lots of people will try to get their two bits in, and if you still want to get your way you have to open your mouth and make a series of sequential, coherent sounds to suggest that the ones rallying voters against you are fools.

In both politics and trading you have to be at least fairly consistent in your arguments, because even though you might be willing to forgive a little slurring of logic on your own part, your opponents will not. (The role of an easy-to-use syllablic alphabet in promoting written records which could be used to confute arguments on false precedent, has also been justly noted as being important, and unique, in Greece; when coins are viewed as 'public documents', the two will coincide, giving a double oomph to our results.) Rationalism follows, or at least is more likely than in places, such as almost every other society on earth in ancient times, where there was no such experience of open quibbling in both trade and government. Open insults, indignation at those insults, and rhetorically slashing arguments back and forth, were essential. It is the summation of dickering. As Aristotle, the greatest codifier of this view, put it some time later:

But it is not worth scrutinizing too seriously the subtleties of mythologizers. Instead, we must find out . . . by cross-questioning those who are prepared to offer arguments . . .

What our argument motivating rationality doesn't demand is any special place for coins. For that we need to turn to the second, and perhaps even more important, part of the move towards rationalism. This was the development of abstraction. Here coins are crucial. Carry out market dealings through gold and, however fancy the deal, however much quibbling and dickering may have gone into it, you're still in the realm of concrete particulars. Replace that gold, which is just money, by coins however, which are not just money but *currency*, and you have an entirely different deal. A coin is something more than it seems. Gold contains its value in itself, but a coin only makes sense for someone who accepts it as an abstracted coding of value. Hold a coin and you're holding something which is both there and not there, for it gets its power only because of a decision made in an often distant city, which however you are accepting even where you are, far away from the source. It is the essence of the island system which saw the Greek cities regularly send out settlement colonies, which remained bound to the home city not officially, but more abstractly, by continually reasserted memory and sentiment. Non-Greeks in the sixth century BC (when that rapid spread of Greek settlements and inter-trading was taking place) had problems with the concept of coins, as evidenced by the fact that archaeologists digging up Greek coins which ended up being traded into regions under Egyptian or Persian rule, find that they have often been left not intact, but hacked at with a chisel to check their purity and weight. For the non-Greeks the notion of currency beyond mere money was too outlandish. They treated coins as oddly shaped bullion, not currency. For them only precious metal of a given weight, what you can see and hold in front of you, made any sense. The habit in many Greek cities of putting designs on the coins that were puns on the city's name (as if Washington DC used a washing machine as its emblem) would also have seemed outlandish to them, but of course such puns – the shield (*Bous*) of Boeotia, the rose (*Rodon*) of Rhodes and many others – naturally arose if you think of coins as encapsulated abstraction.

The point is one of requiring acceptance of two apparent contradictories at once. For anyone but a hard-eyed trader it would be a recipe for woolly-mindedness, just the sort of thing the old myths would be good for; but for someone who is damned well going to cram anything he comes across into a presumed rationalism, that contradiction will have to be taken care of. There is just one way to do this. The two apparently contradictory statements, that 'Ariaxes has turned his chariot left', and 'Ariaxes has turned his chariot right', can only be sensibly combined if you go up a level and report that 'Ariaxes has made a turn'. (It is an elementary point in the sort of logic Aristotle later developed.) Cram the two contradictory attributes of a coin – carrying the mark of this city here, into that city there – together and the only thing that can rationally pop out is an abstraction.

Such abstraction has its comforts for a society moving away from belief in the old supernatural world behind everything. It allows you to get some of the comfort of the old regime without regressing and admitting failure. For coins, being abstract, have a meaning above the simple reality of their material presence, and yet they have this extra-meaning without recourse to the Beyond, without making you go back to the old myths or supernatural stories, but as solid items existing right there before you. That's their duality, all of it – the dickering and the payment, the separated islands and the uniting sea; that's their duality, all wrapped into one.

An example of this rational abstraction is the argument Anaximander gave as to why the earth stayed in place. Here we are at one of the most momentous points in Western intellectual history, the birth of rational, philosophic inquiry. There had at various times been other explanations, all of which seem unconvincing today, from the general theories such as that the Gods made the earth so tired before putting it in place that it has remained exhausted and too tired to move ever since, to the particular ones such as that it was resting on a large and very stable turtle. These explanations are hard to see in action, and hard to argue with. ('But if you believe the world rests on a turtle,' William James is reported to have asked the visitor in his lecture hall, 'what does the turtle rest on?' 'You can't fool me, Mr. James: it's turtles all the way down!') Anaximander's explanation, that it stayed in place because otherwise you have to assume an assymetrical force pulling it to one side, is remarkably sensible. He leaves out beings beyond this observable world who might shake and grab and move things that affect us; indeed he makes a virtue out of explaining the earth's position without them. The explanation is not perfect ('symmetrical to what?' has proved a fertile ground for

speculation since) but extraordinary in making do while leaving the
supernatural out of it. It is the beginning of the concept of nature;
where only rules understandable to man prevail.

The chronology of this explanation is interesting. Anaximander
and the other earliest philosopher-scientist, Thales, did their work at
the beginning of the sixth century BC. The invention and first use of
coins came just a few years earlier, at the end of the previous century,
when these men were coming of age. What's more, the city where
Anaximander and Thales lived was Miletus, a major trading port,
with numerous colonies and lots of trade, travellers, and currency
coming through – what exemplified the curiously linked yet testily
independent doings of so many Greek cities.

Anaximander's detailed theories match that in the way we've now
come to expect. They are also worth looking into for revealing
something of man's move from myth to science. If coins can help
explain the setting up of a detailed science, then their role in more
general social thought is more plausible. Anaximander's central point
seems to have been that there was a universal substance, behind and
backing everything, termed the Indefinite. This is odd until we think
of it as an attempt to give a material image to the possibility of
rational explanation, which also pervades everything. At particular
points, according to Anaximander, the Indefinite would coalesce, or
'thicken', to create the particular substances that we know. This too is
odd until we note that rational explanation only comes out when we
get down to work on it at particular points; it is even less odd if we
think back to what position the Greeks themselves were in: they were
not spread randomly and evenly around the Mediterranean, but
huddled together, in concentrated city-states, those 'frogs and ants'
we met above. The coalescing was even stronger in a trading center,
and Miletus was one of the busiest and most complex of all Greek
trading cities.

In mythology the explanation would have been simple. If a great
city existed, this was because the Gods had chosen its location as the
preferred conduit for their offerings from the Other Side. Not so for
Anaximander. It was created, as anyone could see, as was proven by
the shouts of every trader and Greek-speaking visitor, by the
construction of buildings and piers with profits from the inflowing
wealth; it was created by the actual coalescing of people and goods
and cash from this world right here. There was no need to stray into
the Beyond. The city was what you saw before you. Even the internal
political set-up in Miletus was clearly real, clearly not divine: there

had in the generation or two before been a succession of aristocracy, merchant plutocracy and something of a populist dictatorship, based entirely on the disposition of force, and the arguments between the different factions.

Anaximander's next point is often considered very peculiar. As the Indefinite transformed and solidified into the particular substances we know, he said, it would go on to assure that those created substances would always interact and push against each other in accord with the standards of what was fair and appropriate:

they pay penalty and retribution to each other for their injustice according to the assessment of time.

This quote is, incidentally, the only sentence we have in Anaximander's own words, and indeed the oldest extant sentence surviving from the birth of rational philosophy. (Not a scrap that Thales wrote survives, and everything else we know about Anaximander is from later paraphrases, often by his opponents.) What the quote states is that all the material objects in the world interact in accord with the principles of fair exchange – and that is just the principle we have seen in prices, and personality, and Greek politics. The accord is very close. If the material objects in the world don't act 'justly', if they push and nudge and attempt to take over more than what is appropriate for them, then the other objects around them will get back at them and make sure they go back to acting as they should. It is, as usual, a world of justice, and it is produced, as usual, by quibbling and dickering and no one being willing to put up with less than he deserves.

Only one thing in Anaximander's work is not subject to justice, interchange, malleability; this is the setting in which all those created material objects exist. The earth, air and sea, he said, once created, stay forever. That's good, because it is the one boundary his theory needs to make the analogy complete. Earth, air and sea, in the order they are out there to see, were the indispensable setting necessary for the Greek world to exist as it did too. Everything in Anaximander's theory changes, just as every item in the Greek world changed –coins, goods and political ideas, all being infinitely malleable and exchangeable – except that indispensable setting, which set them both up to change the same.

It is tempting to continue with a full history of Greek thinkers in terms of their use of the three readily mimicked levels of man, city and nature, but that would be more than even the best intentioned of

readers could be asked to bear. Instead only two more of the pre-
Socratics will get the treatment – a restriction sufficient, we might
hope, to show the place of money in holding together these abstract
moves from level to level.

For Pythagoras and his followers the entire world was built up
from numbers; in numbers are to be found:

the fount and root of ever-flowing nature.
(Geoffrey Kirk, *The Presocratic Philosophers*, p. 233)

Sometimes this assumption was well-founded and they succeeded.
Thus in music they managed to show how beautiful chords are really
just mixtures of mathematically simple base tones. Sometimes it was
not so well-founded: their efforts to find the numerical constituents of
certain lines in a triangle let loose those strange objects called
irrational numbers, which mathematicians for the next 2,000 years
would be unable to handle, and which the Pythagoreans could just
gaze at, wondering what they had wrought. Yet still they didn't stop:
the Pythagoreans were going to see numbers at the root of all objects
– music, lines; the mind, city and cosmos too they declared – come
what may.

This is suspiciously familiar. Pythagoras didn't grow up in Miletus,
but he did come from Samos, just off-shore, which was one of the
main trade rivals to the old city of Anaximander. He lived later in the
century, but not so much so that coins were not still a new and much
remarked upon powerful human construction. The reason for
thinking coins were somehow at the base of Pythagoras's numerical
theory even though he talked about objects on all the several levels –
soul to cosmos – is that those objects themselves are not exact and
mathematical. Coins are. Also coins encode, group together, the
similarities between those several levels, for all the reasons we've
already seen. For someone holding that in mind, puzzling out the
numerical bases of reality was then a task he would be priorly
convinced would be likely to succeed – since he knew the numerically
exact base of 'price' could be puzzled out for any material object.

If you were from Samos you would have experience of seeing the
role of coined money on the city and regional level too. City politics
was dominated by publicly displayed dirty-dealing in this period:
landed aristocrats were pushed out, the merchants of the city were
buying their way up, and, especially when Pythagoras was there, the
unpleasant tyrant Polycrates was pushing his way past even them.

There were big public works, paid for in coin, Aristotle informs us; there were mercenaries and control of the neighboring islands too. That the changes at the political level were felt to be monetarily based is suggested by the fact that after Polycrates's gory death (by the Persians, whom he was lured to visit, neatly enough, by the promise of yet more money) his successor promised to end dissent by passing out Polycrates's great accumulated wealth. He reneged, of course, for he needed money, in the shape of those mathematically precise coins, to make more of everything he wanted. Although Pythagoras by then was long gone, having become fed up and emigrated to southern Italy, he had seen enough to make it unlikely that he would be surprised if he heard. The goings-on in Samos didn't force Pythagoras to come up with the theories he did – lots of other citizens there came up with nothing – but suddenly to get the idea about exact numbers hiding inside all things without any such help is perhaps more than we can expect any individual to do.

Although the details of Pythagoras's project couldn't be worked out in ancient time – it's too hard – the program he set continued with a certain effect. Some of the holdovers are small, such as our use of 'even' to describe half our numbers. This dates back to Pythagoras, and carries the notion of there being lots of little '2s' in such numbers, even though on the surface we cannot see them there. Some of the consequences have been more important however, such as the notion that a few simple axioms can explain all mathematics and generally all of science. This, cranked up to the human level, is the basis for those general principles in the US Constitution: the Enlightenment men who wrote it were searching for axioms in politics that were just as good as the axioms in Pythagorean-descended mathematics. There could be no possible visible evidence for such natural rights, but then there was no possible visible evidence for the full range of Pythagoras's thought either.

The final thinker will be the one we came in on. Democritus held that everything was composed of atoms: solid, massy, tiny objects; infinitely small, and always attempting to whir through the void. They are all made of the same substance, though it is shaped in slightly different ways, and depending on the shape, when they thwack together sometimes they will stick, and sometimes they will just rebound and continue on their way. From the ones that stick all material objects in the universe are composed: mountains, philosophers, sandals, you name it.

The similarities to Pythagoras are clear. Replace numbers by atoms and there, but for some vagueness about what controls the whirring, you are. It has advantages over Pythagoras, too, because numbers, though interesting, do not weigh anything, and so however many you pile together you would still have problems creating the weighty material objects – the mountains, philosophers, etc. – that the numbers are supposed to make. There are defenses you can make for Pythagoras (in his full system numbers only suggest inner natures, and don't constitute them) and there is also the point that Democritus, coming late in the fifth century BC, was also responding to some technical problems left by the intervening thinkers. But still there is that overall similarity to Pythagoras, and also the fact that Democritus insisted his system could be used to explain not just chunky material things like mountains and philosophers, but individual thought, and politics, and even cosmology too.

And the role of coins? Their place in grouping similar explanations on these different levels remain the same, yet there is also, in the time of Democritus, a century or more after the other thinkers we've considered, something else, very curious, that was happening to them. Coins suddenly started to shrink. Early ones had been made big enough for big purchases. A standard weight through the sixth century was twelve grams for a coin – about the same as an American half dollar or British ten pence piece. Although there were a few exceptions, it was only in the middle of the fifth century that they began generally to change. Coins started to be minted not just for bulk payments but for daily transactions. And since they were weight-based, the only way for the denominations to go down was for the coins themselves to shrink.

In Athens, where the twelve-gram coin represented an average week's wage, the standard small coin had been the *triobol*. This was two grams, a sixth of the large coin, and considered fair service for a day's jury service. That's small, but there was much worse to come. First there was the *trihemiobol* (one and a half *obol*) at one gram, and then the *obol* itself, about 0.68 grams. That is a very small amount of metal. It is so small that is could be conveniently carried around in the mouth, a habit Aristophanes used to benefit in the *Wasps*, where Lysistratus substitutes a fish scale for one, and Philocleon, not noticing the difference, pops it into his mouth as usual. Such problems did not stop the wild descent. Below the individual *obol* there was created the *hemiobol* (half *obol*), then the *trihemitetartemorion*, and finally, stamped and with all the official insignia on it, as one can see at the British Museum if one stands very close to the one in the back room and peers right down, the masterpiece of coin miniaturization, the Athenian *tetartemorion*: all 0.16 grams of it.

Democritus was likely to come across these coins, intrusive and noteworthy as lap-held computers are today perhaps, for he lived in Abdera, on the northern edge of the Aegean, and while that was an important trading city it was not at all as important or powerful as Athens, and was increasingly, in the mid and later fifth century, coming under Athenian sway. For a country that had had an independent coinage this was a mess. In the previous century, shortly after Abdera was founded (it had been a settlement colony for Teos, 250 miles further south) it had produced the distinctive giant *octodrachm* coin, thirty-gram monsters, and from the beginning of the fifth century it continued to produce its own coins, with its distinctive griffin symbol, whenever it could. This was not very often. First they had had to produce Persian coinage, then when they were freed of that in 478 BC they became loaded with Athenian coins, though they were still able to produce some of their own coins – but only until 432 BC, when Athens insisted that its standards must be followed for all silver coins, and all Abderan money became worthless until it could be produced in the weights for that standard. Englishmen who remember the experience of the pound in their pocket seeming to carry an intrusive American IMF official on it, or Americans remembering their dollar seemingly controlled by oil sheiks, will understand how deeply the external control of currency could cut. Democritus was especially aware of all these coinly doings, for he was from a wealthy enough family to have had his own name on one of the Abderan coins when as a young man he served a term of office. What Pythagoras had had to take as an abstraction – the exactly numerical coin-like base of reality – Democritus, with coins everywhere, representing and creating all bonds of polity and empire, existent from the barely visible metal *trihemitetartemorions* on up, could base directly on a material solid.

It would be nice if a statue survived showing Democritus holding his text on atoms proudly in front of him in one hand, while glancing with raised eyebrows and a knowing smile at a tiny coin he held out of the way in the other hand. But archaeology is not so kind. The researcher has to guess, and if honest should say where he's guessing. I'm honest. My confidence in the evidence is highest at the beginning of this Greek section, where I make the points about money being both a sign and encoded maintainer of abstractive rationalism; I'm fairly confident about the role of money in the general approach of theorists such as Anaximander and Pythagoras, if not in their detailed points; and I'm really just speculating for fun by the time we get to Democritus. An image that's useful is one suggested by Anaximander, that the earth is a great cylinder, rotating in darkest space. Let us imagine man and all his doings at any instant spread on the outside. Then all that we as historical investigators can do is shine a narrow light beam on to the turning cylinder. A small portion lights up, and the interlinked causes we wish to uncover will have to start from there.

After Democritus the most innovative development of Greek coins was over – and so was the most innovative period in their analyzing of physical matter. There were to be ingenious combinations of the old theories, and much fresh work on ordering our knowledge of matter, but nothing really new about the stuff inside it. This would only be expected if the original theories had been a recodification of the general setting. In a culture that did not encourage thinkers to touch or handle messy things in the real world, there would be no chance for what we would consider the facts of physics or chemistry to speak. Ideas could be imputed to the outside world. But the material world, not listened to closely enough, could not speak back.

III. It was to be a long, long time before atoms came back into fashion again, though when it happened it was a very sudden thing. In the mid sixteenth century there were a few reprintings of the old atomists kicking around, though hardly anyone did anything with them. By the early seventeenth century, though, they were the assumed basis of all the most advanced thinkers, and by later in that century they had taken over so completely that the thought of any other theory of matter was preposterous.

What makes this sudden re-emergence especially odd is that it all happened with almost no scientific evidence to back it. The great seventeenth-century scientists came up with almost no conclusions that depended specifically on atoms, yet despite this lack of necessity they insisted that atoms were the necessary parts of the matter they were dealing with. Social philosophers also started assuming atoms or atom-like entities as their first principles – Hobbes especially; think also of Leibniz with his silently synchronized windowless monads – with even less verifiable cause than the scientists. And throughout, the accounts of atoms doubled up as accounts of people on the old Greek model again: the atoms were held to be solid, autonomous, have precise boundaries, be tied to nothing, intermingle only by furious collision, and all the rest.

It might seem that thinkers had just started mimicking humans again, looking into the social world for their inspiration, but that will not quite do as an explanation, because humans can do many things, and a few centuries earlier the reflected picture you would have obtained would have been all clumpy, not separate – the Church and bonds of religion would have seen to that. What the new atoms did mimic rather was a particular type of human being: that poor creature, much abused by historians, once known simply as *l'honnête homme*, but who has since been given an alternative, less esteemed name: this is our old friend, the *bourgeois*.

When exactly he originated is a matter of much debate. The northern Italian city-states some time in the fifteenth century were once considered the standard spot, but as historians for reasons of affection or distaste have been keen to pluck him out in every period they can, various sightings, sometimes even important ones, are reported earlier. One can join the tale at any point, and our interest will start us in the seventeenth century, where a certain threshold point seems to have been reached. It was clear in ideas, with the new science, and it also seems to have been a threshold in sheer numbers of the new bourgeois and their doings, since while some of their paper tools had been around a long time (bills of exchange were used in several Italian cities in the thirteenth century) and increasingly important in the sixteenth century, it was only late in the seventeenth century, in England at least, that the very first general issue paper bank notes were printed – the ancestors of all our dollar bills and pound notes. The point is generally put as noting that while a sleeper from the main medieval period awakening in the late 1500s would have not been too suprised at what he saw, the same man groggily stirring in the early 1700s would feel he was in a different world. In between, something very important happened. Still, the dates should be treated as suggestive, and not exclusive.

In his doings, and the world he tried to surround himself with, clothe himself by, our seventeenth-century bourgeois matched the properties of that century's modern atom. The double entry bookkeeping he used in his business made him be accurate, precise, concerned with the most petty details of incomings and outgoings; it required him to size up any other creature not by what emotion or impulse might suggest but simply by what it might do for these numbers he was arranging. All that new paper money around in this period, all the easy procedures for drawing up bills of exchange and promissory notes, were there waiting to carry out these precise and rather impersonal exchanges. The new laws of inheritance (before the seventeenth-century French law generally transferred all goods direct to the blood successor) gave him all the grief of making wills, deciding who got what, having to count up his worldly possessions with the greatest accuracy, to forestall the certain arguments about how unfairly he was doing the division. If he wished to go out there was the new theater with its dramatic unities, showing such a world of clear, separate entities in interaction, far more satisfactory than the old traditional horseplay; if he wanted to read in the evening, under his quilt, nightcap on, there was the comforting philosophy of Descartes or his popularizers to go through, showing that the mind began as a blank ledger, to be filled up by proper accounting practices, although safely guaranteed to come up with the old, satisfying certitudes in the end.

What carried over from level to level was only the pure and exact interlinkings suggested by money – and those similarly abstract properties of autonomous collision and accumulation that so many thinkers were finding in their new atoms.

Each one, in the appropriate realm, was increasingly being held to account for existence on every level. In money, the growth of bourgeois accumulation on the individual level was matched by mercantilism on the state level. It is clear in all Colbert's well-known, and at the time innovative, homilies: that only money makes a state strong, that competition between states is at heart a 'Money Wars', and that no one gains without another one losing – an early and neat summation of zero-sum accounting. The individual money-man and the state as a whole were no longer tied to land or tradition, but became free-floating, autonomous beings, interacting in accord with the cool logic of money alone. In atoms, the similarity between the several levels was a commonplace of up-to-date thinkers. Human individuals composed of swarming yet properly arranged atom particles, at one level of Hobbes's work, went on to create the proper Commonwealth out of similarly swarming yet properly arranged individuals at a higher level. Leibniz's monads worked at both levels in a similar way; Locke's clearly interlinked simple ideas in the mind were readily seen as the right model for clearly interlinked simple principles in the state; and even Newton had the tiny atoms within us, the larger parts of the body, and even the planets in their orbits, all combine and separate by what he held to be precise, and deeply similar, laws.

What we have is not only a ranking of moneys, and a ranking of atoms, but a similarity in the way the two rankings worked out. The money on each level was scurrying around like the atoms on each level. Reasons for the similarity are not hard to find. It is the old trick of commissioning a toady to sculpt your portrait, and then remarking, with pleasure and surprise, at how noble your features are therein found to be. Why should the private interests of atomic man produce concord when heaped together to become the public interests of atomic society? Because the physical world, produced by heapings of physical atoms, was clearly solid and in order too. The very origins of the new science support it: algebra was much developed to meet bankers' needs in early Renaissance times, and so the science which later developed using those mathematical concepts would quite naturally match for a while the doings of financially dealing individuals – both the humans and the algebraic variables x and y being solid, atom-like entities, with exact, impersonal forces working between them.

Above all, the seventeenth-century atom stackings and money stackings were linked because it was felt that both were but aspects of the mind of God. The bourgeois making money was a devout creature, humbly residing in God's world. The atomists who had such a problem showing that their atoms would whir in synchronization also resolved their problem by declaring that God had set the atoms moving in the right way. He could do so because the atoms at all the different levels were within Him, or at least under His sway. This is why the Laws of Nature and the Laws of God were held to be the same. It was also this similarity that later made it so easy to have the atoms continue working on several levels in what was no longer the inside of God's mind, but the natural world alone: a novel end-game twist in the ancient struggle of Mammon against God.

What we are getting is something like the relation between individuals – that hesitant interlinking of separate beings – which we saw with the Greeks. It is not exactly the same: the eastern Mediterranean of the fifth and sixth centuries BC was not Western Europe of the seventeenth century AD. But is was close enough, at the level of abstraction we're interested in, to set up this climate of intellectual atomism. The overlap was extensive. Not only was there physical atomism, but there was also, in seventeenth-century Europe, a reassertion of the axiomatic method, in almost every realm of knowledge people could bear to write about: natural philosophers, social philosophers, legal philosophers and philospher philosophers increasingly assembled their work in this style: sometimes profoundly, sometimes not. Such axiomatization, as we saw with Pythagoras, readily corresponds with this particular human individual: the axioms themselves are hard, absolute, and not to be tampered with, like autonomous individuals; and the larger world the insightful philosopher shows them to belong to is also what an image of such individuals presents, for it is created entirely by the axioms' proper combination.

The notion of axioms did not have to be totally developed anew. They had been on tap, stored away, in Euclid all this time. Also there were useful translations of Archimedes in the sixteenth century. But their existence in books would not alone be enough to make them emerge again at this time. Something outside was pulling, and this was the attitude that reality, the true nature of what was, was to be found by starting with small kernels, be they atoms, or human individuals, or axioms, and then working out the details of their combination to create all else.

For the greatest of all the century's thinkers yet another technique that Pythagoras would not have been surprised at was pulled out too: this was the break-up of all that could be described mathematically into certain very simple, basic 'numbers'. When schoolchildren first learn calculus today they are taught to think of the symbol dx as an indication of a certain infinite series, or perhaps as the possibility of a certain proof procedure. But this is not how Newton used it when he taught the subject to himself. For him (and Leibniz, too) dx was a real object, something of a little number, smaller than other numbers admittedly, but existing in its own right. Those infinitesimals that were there if you hunted small enough in mathematics were a fair counterpart to the atoms that the corpuscular theory declared you would find if you hunted small enough in matter. The fact that Newton was able to get extraordinary use out of these infinitesimals was an added treat.

Where seventeenth-century concepts appeared which were entirely beyond what the Greeks had, it is interesting to note that they might have been linked to specifically seventeenth-century social forms too. What is a mathematical function, for example, but a summary of what one of the new joint-stock companies of the time was doing? The Greeks had neither, but seventeenth-century Europeans had both. Such companies were entities, treated legally as individuals, which although they had complex internal doings also had the wonderful property of being able to give at any instant a simple read-out of their current worth in exact numerical form. This is, of course, what mathematical functions do, expecially the first ones Newton used so brilliantly, which were of the simple form $f(t)$. The joint stock ˙companies, with their double-entry bookkeeping and their instant cash values, could be seen as huge examples, on the loose for everyone to see, of mathematical functions at work. The new individual, defined quite sufficiently by his ever-present cash or status or some other exact, logically separable value, was but the same, geared down to an appropriately tinier level.

It might seem odd that a science which is socially based should also turn out to be true. But at the moment of setting up the bases of a discipline it is neither true nor false. Almost any set of notions is possible – as Needham has shown so eloquently with China, where field concepts entered early on into disciplines where we would not think they were appropriate. The seventeenth-century European science pioneers took their foundations from a range of sources, which often included, naturally enough, abstract properties of the society around them. Often this was a big mistake, as with the cockeyed notions seventeenth-century chemistry became loaded with, but sometimes it turned out to be fruitful – as with mathematical physics, and its notions of abstract space, function, and all the rest. The power of science is that where a 'good' choice has been made it will grow, and where a poor start has been made it will flounder. This is why the hunt for social foundations becomes less sensible as a scientific discipline developes: internal logic, and accord with facts, take over instead. This is also why scientists who have embraced the Seductress of philosophy but escaped intact note, sadly, that while it takes pencil, paper and a waste-bin to equip a top-notch department of mathematics, it is possible to equip a philosophy department with the first two alone.

What the reasons were for the increasing numbers of bourgeois individuals in Europe at this time has been the subject of much debate. Suggestions have ranged from changing means of production to the internal history of ideas, new ship technology, political quirks, new weapons technology, declining interest rates (which increased supplies of venture capital); even that it was necessary to prepare the way for the Prussian state a century and a half later. With the exception of the last one they all have some merit. Our approach spares us having to choose between them, let alone having to describe the great number of other events in this period not immediately related to our atom-like heroes. Even where they overlapped – thus the autonomous individual postulated in French wills was sometimes felt to be a hierarchical mimicking of the autonomous Louis in his wigs at Versailles – the other events later separated enough for our selective narrative here to make sense. All we're really doing is hŏming in on that one particular group in which we, struggling individuals all, have a particular interest. Had an immense and hairy creature from the direction of the star Sirius flapped over with leathery wings and swallowed the earth on December 31, 1699, so ending human history there, we with our retrospective curiosity about merchants would not be here, and so a fair account of the 1600s up until the Great Swallowing would be one giving more space to kings. As it is, what our study shows is that it was money that was the indispensable carrier of the new individualist meanings in society.

Other devices could in theory have done the job, but suffered a consistent fault. To take the prime example, the clocks and other machines that had become increasingly popular by the seventeenth-century also seemed to carry the key notion that the power to force movements could be internal, and unhooked from external authority: every working machine, clanking along magically by itself, no people or God or King's regent inside to drive it, showed the possibility of individual humans sojourning through life alone, or at least in their own self-selected group. The limitation, however, was that while some thinkers would imaginatively enter into this device, many other humans would not. Why should they? It is quite possible to admire a machine from outside, just looking at the results of what it does; it's even possible to operate a machine without entering into the rules by which it works, since it has knobs and buttons and other controlling devices on the outside, which one only has to turn or push to get the clanking thing to go. And pressing buttons and turning knobs does not a mechanical or individualist approach to life necessarily make. It's a different thing entirely; you can stand back, separate and untouched, while it clanks away. The misunderstanding is persistent, and extends at least to those American State Department officials who suggested that selling rationally built warplanes to the Shah would make the users of those planes into little fermenters of American rational individualism within Iran.

Money is different. It is a machine which if thoroughly used requires us to be on the inside of it. It's just not possible to go through the motions of using ledgers and bills of exchange and double-entry and all the rest without being, at least for the duration, a cool, autonomous node – an individual, impermeable atom – around which this money can swirl. These handles and knobs are ones that can only be reached from the inside. You would have to be very obstinate to mistake them. And who wants to go through life being obstinate? The more that money suffused through the European economy, the more that the meaning it encapsulated was dug in. Certainly it coincided with the new attitudes in Britain and the Netherlands, and merchants everywhere were the least superstitous of folk. That's why we select money as the binding cement of the new attitudes: maintaining, or encoding, or even propelling along that curious new individual – which the right turn of our rotating cylinder of causes shows was being formed.

IV.   But the bourgeois was not the only individual we can see coming into being in this era. There was also the wage-earning individual. Before the early modern period hardly anyone, anywhere, received wages. Not rich people nor the predecessors of our *honnêtes hommes*, who received rents or the proceeds of their transactions, and certainly not peasants, who lived outside of the money economy most of the time, especially in their daily doings. In the seventeenth-century, though, that had clearly begun to change. Many words associated with wage-work appeared for the first time in English: 'employ' as a noun of condition, 'job' to mean a limited piece of work, and even *'unimploied'* for those who weren't receiving any wages. By the early industrial period in the following century the division of incomes into the three categories of land-rent, profit, and now wages was part of economic orthodoxy.

For each system of payment there was a different assumption about time. The upper classes who lived off land rent had it the best. Land was eternal, and so they, sharing in it, got to be a little bit eternal too. Land also would always be there, and always be needed, and so provided its wealth automatically, effortlessly, without need for the owner of the rights to that land to have to do anything.

Those who lived off speculation or professional work accepted that they were one level down, since the nature of their incomes brought them necessarily closer to the messy and exhausting flux. Their money was produced by events that existed in the realm of active time – shipping futures, legal services – and which also demanded an effort, a slightly demeaning entering of that contemporary flux, on the earner's part. They would live in spurts and jumps of a few years down to even just months – the scale of time which it took a shipping scheme to work itself out, or a court case to be assembled and worked through – and their payments would be a sign of what happened in those fragments of time. When I happily carry a check for a six-month project in my pocket back from the exchange I am also carrying a device for reflecting on my recent life as having been plopped into a six-month length.

The wage-earner was squeezed into even smaller fragments of time. What he did took little time, could be accounted for in hours or even minutes, and was accordingly paid for by wages that were based on the hour or, for some piece-work, bare minutes.

Think of what the different systems reveal. If you know that I have perpetual rights to a property you learn nothing about how I spend my time. The land rights are greater even than an individual life. It is like aiming a searchlight at a long brick wall: all you see on the ground behind it is a continuous, undifferentiated shadow. If, however, you know that I earn my money in transactions that take a year or so to pull off, then you know a bit more: the searchlight of knowledge about my salary gives a horizontal shadow that stops, reveals a gap, starts again, reveals another gap after a while, and repeats this. The broader divisions of my life are revealed to you. It doesn't give me as much privacy as the landlord, but at least within those lengths I am invisible to you, and what I do in each length is private to myself, and not made clear in my salary. Such privacy over fairly long lengths of time is one of the pleasures of salaried jobs, as business consultants, who get such resentment when they try to make salaried employees account for each week or even day of their time, are aware.

The wall that represents the wage-earner is even more divided, split up into individual bricks, held separated from each other by little dowels perhaps. The searchlight shone at that wall produces no large sections of shadow, but rather outlines each constituent brick. There is no privacy. Every action at work is made clear on the outside, as notated in those accounts of daily or weekly wages. There is also no knowledge for those on the inside. Being so divided, the doing of any of the paid-for tasks gives no information about the arrangement of the whole. That knowledge is contained higher up, stored in the ledgers and rules of the man or management group which pays the wages.

Now reverse the argument. Suppose that the worker wants to get out of this public, minutely controlled world. It would be very difficult, because the division of his life into those dribs and drabs of time has been encapsulated in those dribs and drabs of wages that he depends on. That is not just a matter of being broke on Friday morning and looking forward, keenly, to the wage packet that afternoon. Rather it is the certainty that this is going to happen, and the automatic building up of graspable time into tiny intervals of just weeks or days that this produces. Even if the wage-earner does try to think on larger time-scales, where will the knowledge be to control or create a new job? It certainly won't be found in any of the tasks he or his colleagues have been doing till then.

It is all somehow the bourgeois dream gone wrong. Both were increasingly recognized in the individualism of the seventeenth-century, called into being by hiving off from the more joined-up groups of before. Yet for one of them, through the medium of wages, that individuality became a means of being held on the bottom, under control.

The arrangement is a convenient one. There never had to be any conscious planning in this: it was the natural way a power system working through the individual would come out. By everyone acting out what their pay system suggests, the system will be stable overall. No one has to repress anything. The top people get the nicest reward, hovering up there just on the edges of eternity. The middle people will stay in line working hard to become the top people, for part of their goal is to extend the intervals of time in which they can appear to be effortless, and so any fussing or revealing of the often dirty doings they have to come across in their climb would obviate that partial success. And the people at the bottom, the waged workers, will be non-rebellious, having, at least from their jobs and pay, neither incentive, nor opportunity, nor the knowledge to object. There is no slit into past time through which they can see the origins of their miserable position. All is accepted, as truce lines long after a war are accepted. It is not a question of the job itself. A factory is a complex thing, if you consider it as a point in the economic system, controlling purchasings, transforming material, hooked up to arrange-ments for marketing or further use. When it becomes not complex is when the constituents in it are divided up so that they have no active link with the whole. That is not inherent in factories, just frequent in societies – and when it occurs it is what those money wages, supplied in divided-up drops, will match and help maintain.

The embrace is strong, and over time was easily generalized. If for the wage-earner the inside of his job tasks are on display, there for public observation, then wouldn't it be fitting for the insides of his body to be open to the outside world too? Such a physical enactment of what's held to be the truth system in a society would not be unique to industrial times. The code of civility in courtly behaviour that developed after the Religious Wars (it was the era when using the fork was first encouraged, and spitting at table and picking fights there was discouraged) was often explained as being the right thing because it matched the new violence-reducing political truth standards of the time. For the industrial wage-earners, the coarser they are – the more their ethos allows of burping, farting, spitting, etc. – the more comfortable their higher ups can be, for individuals revealing in their body actions what is inherently produced inside seem to be showing that they match, accept and fit in to that system where their jobs are divided up so as to be directly or indirectly on display. There is a vast literature, of comfort to the middle class, which uses these stereotypes of the workers as coarse people, dominated by their insides, on the verge at every moment – statements interrupted by a sniff, or cough, or spit – of letting it come out. Unfortunately it can also feel natural to the wage-earner too, whence that other literature, and today popular television shows and films, which are accepted by the wage-earners and show 'honest' working life as one where a man is not ashamed of revealing what's inside of him. In a bar he belches when he feels like belching, smacks his best friend over the shoulder when he wants to show his binding affection to him, and all the rest.

The more respectable classes would go to very great lengths to stop themselves from doing this, or being seen doing this. What is inside is to be kept there, in the dark and private, where it is under personal control, and not let out. Let someone else start supervising your insides and who knows where it might end. It's the slippery slope to the wage world. Sometimes human physiology allows this to be done without much problem. Spitting and yelling can be restrained by keeping the mouth closed. Sniffs can be controlled with thoughtful advance action of a kleenex. Smacking, whether of friends or foes, can be restrained by trained inhibition of the shoulder muscles. But sometimes it is more difficult. Humans being descended from certain radially symmetric worm-like creatures, we still have a central tube-like cavity in which food must be placed, generally to be ground and properly salivated, before it can be brought further into the body. In this mouthly spot, half-in, half-out, control easily falters. Rules accordingly have had to be harsher. First of all there's no eating outside: no apples munched on streets (the standard film convention announcing a street urchin), no sandwiches finished off on the walk. Then, even at the table, that which is being worked over in the buccal cavity must be manipulated in such a way as to suggest that it is not being worked over; indeed that it is not even there. There can be no gulping, loud chewing, tongue slapping, squelching, slurping or swishing. As the mouth, doubling up as it does as the near-final stretch of our speech transmission channel is inherently megaphone-shaped, any error, any slip, will be amplified to be broadcast for all to hear. Nor is there much space to carry out the secret food mangling, no possibility of stretching the jaws wide to give some more angle for the tongue to twist, the cheeks to contort. Visual revelation would be as bad as oral. All must be done in the small volume, only a few cubic inches, within the firmly lip-sealed cavity. The art of containment is difficult. But if it were not taught, not insisted upon despite childhood protest, despite these physiological constraints, what horrible revelations there would be.

Orgasm presents an especial problem for the respectable classes. It would be better if it could be suppressed all together, but this is difficult. One compromise would be to somehow create little mini-orgasms, tiny body-suffusing thrill experiences, and show that one is brave enough, tough enough, in control of the self enough, to be able to experience those mini-bursts without revealing anything on the outside. This is, one can't help but imagining, what that fuss in respectable circles about the aesthetic experience, the cathartic thrust and thrill of looking at fine art or listening to fine music, is all about. Some people would see a great painting and be so moved that they would shriek. That shows weakness. That shows an inability to keep what should be on the inside down in there where it belongs. The proper thing, as we might imagine a married or courting couple doing perhaps, is to stroll slowly through the art gallery, to turn and stare at a great painting together and then for the woman, without breathing deeply, without shuddering or giving any other sign of physical overwhelming, to say that that was one of the finest aesthetic experiences she has ever had. The man, also demonstrating his strict discipline, making a point of looking unexcited, controlling even any possible untoward flair of the nostrils, will state, solemnly, measuredly, that it has been a maximal cathartic experience for him too. They can talk about the impact, pass it back and forth in one terse statement after another, and everyone on the outside, everyone who understands how incredibly wonderful that Art had been, will know what shuddering joy they are really passing back and forth, and so be able to marvel at their control. The history of fine art and its audience in the past few centuries suggests that all too often it was supported just to have something to demonstrate this containment of the maximal experience a person is capable of.

As with the bodies, so with the self-chosen organizations of those bodies. If workers bodies should be open to viewing and their jobs should be open to viewing, then certainly any of their larger assemblages should be kept permanently cut open for us all to see too. This has meant, historically, that for non-wage-earners from the lowest salaried clerks on up, unions have been felt to be something that was just not right. What are workers doing getting together privately, secretly, without public observation and control anyway? They're supposed to be divided, rule-following obedient creatures, as their wages try to show. And then what's all this about their being able to decide things under their own initiative? Unions shouldn't be able to boss people around, make decisions about them. The cheek of it. Only we, in the business world, should be able to.

Executives get to keep closed up, get to have a large private space for decision that is closed to the outside's inspection, because they are that other kind of impenetrable atom, the lucky kind, the one that in the modern development of the individual was associated with those who gave the orders, not those who received them. He keeps that property whatever happens. Let him swell till he is a vast being, a large corporation, containing thousands of little workers within him, and yet still he remains an atom. Imagine what would happen if that happened literally, a businessman swollen dirigible-like, so large that his skin was taut and translucent, all the little workers visible floating and scrabbling around in there. You would not, if well brought up, make comments about how 'I personally don't mind girth in my friends'; you would not try to sneak a glance through the translucent skin; you would not let your children do so either. They might be tempted at first, mischievously playing around with the great man's loose tuxedo bib to see what's underneath, but with enough practice on the hiding of what goes inside at the dinner table at home, they will accept the principle. What happens inside an atom, inside even the dominion of an extended and – to be honest – unduly large atom, is to be a mystery, a privacy, left up to the atom alone to deal with.

That has been the attitude necessary for the acceptance of what we call private enterprise, especially in the form achieved in its pre-welfare state peak, and associated with the industrial organization of power sources such as the steam engine. All those workers, whom simple-minded observers might think were members of the public, with rights and powers, were actually just constituents of one large thing, which, by its nature, by the credit we gave it, engulfed them into a dark and impermeable atom, from within which no sound should be heard. There was little connection with the original notion of the corporation, developed by mediaeval canon lawyers, of it being an association of individuals united by a shared and self-chosen purpose, such as worshippers, or a guild, or a university. The original etymology held, of a grand *corpus*, or body, but now that body was the top businessman's alone. The insides of such a body, as of any body, were the affair of its owner and on one else. The several levels neatly merged. This was the attitude that allowed the late nineteenth-century US Supreme Court to make those decisions holding that where the Constitution said 'No person shall be . . . deprived of life, liberty, or property, without due process of law . .' what was really meant was that businessmen should be allowed to do whatever they wanted with their workers, their insides, their selves.

The generalized feeling is that workers are muscle. A body politic needs muscle, so it needs workers. But muscle only works, makes sense, if it correlates closely with its task. That's why it's thought to be very, very wrong for someone with a simple job, like a theater stagehand, to earn $50,000 in a year. A shareholder in the company that owns the land which the theater has to pay rent for can earn more than that, but that's different. He's in a whole different realm, where knowledge, fore-planning, cleverness in rigging the game, and all other aspects of the autonomous use of money are allowed. Workers must only get paid for just what their physical movements are. That's what wages correspond to. And pushing stage equipment around is not $50,000 worth of movement.

With the individual who grants wages having such control over his own insides, he also has a possible way to gain some of that freedom from time which the established upper classes have. The landed rich were always very careful to arrange their life so that the proper male heirs would marry and have legitimate children with the appropriately rich females. Their visiting rituals and courtship rituals and methods of ensuring that only the proper individuals would be the subject of marriageable attention were all there, as the biologist might put it, to ensure that favored packets of sperm would be placed in such a setting that once they had gestated and grown into new human beings they would do nothing but repeat the process, pass on the surrounding heritage, and ensure that the subsequent generation of sperm were properly placed too. It is not especially romantic, but it is consoling. For these properly handled sperm become the old man's immortality claim. If the businessman could somehow do the same he would get to be immortal too – a welcome treat since the existence of free-acting businessmen went along with the notion that

God could no longer be trusted to be there to do the job for you.

Think back then to that impolite close-up peering at the grossly swollen businessman, the thousands of scurrying tiny workers who make up his Body Industrial just visible inside. They, and above all their properly scurrying motion, can be his sperm. Make sure they continue on into the future – the workers in the factory for the literal-minded, the arrangement of funds and money investments over distant workers for the more abstractly minded – and through that intermediary, you the businessman, as the carrier of the workers now, as the large Atom containing them in the impermeable depths within you, will have the honor of surviving along with. The material constituents, the mere bodies that happen to make up the workers you're controlling now, are unimportant. They're going to die anyway. It's the arrangement that counts. That's what you encompass, and can guarantee heaving on into the future. This has become dogma. When Sir John Harvey-Jones, hefty and blunt then-chairman of ICI, Britain's largest chemical company, was asked in a BBC interview ('the Money Makers', February 1986) what he said to the charges that he was making thousands of workers unemployed, many of whom wouldn't get a chance of working again, the great man patiently replied that that was not the point. He was there, he said, befuddled that the interviewer couldn't understand, to arrange things so that ICI could survive for decades, maybe even centuries, into the future.

It is a secular consolation, but one with that distinctive seventeenth-century touch, which puts it beyond the earlier Renaissance individual's style of hope for survival. Those were based more on the hope of producing a unique work of art, whose impetus came from a uniqueness within. There might be problems in extracting and solidifying that uniqueness into the outside world – the tribulations which make all the diaries and confessions and satires and portraits of that era so delightful for us – but that step to the outer world, where all was solid or at least publicly viewable, was indispensable. Cellini without his efforts to make his ideas solid sculpture would not be Cellini. Where else could post-death survival possibly take place? The variant *honnête homme* approach, though, which Sir John so earnestly proposes, is one where an individual is more opaque inside, and it is only the properties of that inside which have to be passed on. If no one ever gets to see the inner workings, that's fine. They have little right to be poking around in your space, anyway.

There's an interesting question of causality with this new bourgeois privacy, this acceptance of impermeable atoms with permanently shrouded internal volume. It corresponds with the main epistemological change of the seventeenth century so closely that many thinkers have worried themselves silly trying to figure out which side came first. Was it philosophy that helped the new approach, producing the patches of allowed emptiness necessary for our economically important individuals to grow? Or was it the other way round, with new economic relations encouraging the philosophy to sustain them? The question is noteworthy not just for European history but more generally, since the philosophical system from which the change was made was of the sort that has dominated most humans minds through most of history.

The old universe, on display almost anywhere you looked in sixteenth-century Europe, had been one where everything, especially human intentions, was connected up. There was me here, and you there, and while between us there might look to be just empty air, in fact there was a strong gloopy sheet – the all-connecting backdrop world – through which direct links between us could be made. Everything was embedded in it, like scattered raisins in a large flat sheet of dough. Many people still easily think that way:

The Force is the energy field created by all living things; it binds the galaxy together.
(Alec Guinness in 'Star Wars', 1977)

It is what provided that linking of all human events we saw in the case of Reagan and Nicaragua, and in the astrological consolations of readers of the popular newspapers. The difference is that today most of us know it's not really true, or at least not true enough to act on consciously. But back in the sixteenth century, religion, magical practices and astrology made sense to everyone, since all those practices could use that connecting thing to spread their effects from place to place. There were no gaps, holes or rips: no possibility of private, unobserved space.

Also, back then, it was not man who worked that sheet. Men could pray to it, or try to figure out astrological fortunes from peering at it, but they could not leap up and run around in it. This is why usury was so bad. It assumed that something which man made – money – could increase all by itself. But that was heresy. Men are miserable sinners. The objects they make, such as money, cannot go into that other, magical realm up above, where all sources of increase are controlled.

Similarly it was wrong for men to try to assemble enough money so they could then live without labor, just collecting interest off an investment income. That would make their future life easy – and man had no right to attempt to run the future. Only the thing Up There could. Getting ease from purchase of land or serfs might be okay, since those were made by God, and stayed under His control. But not from pulling coins – *man's* coins – out of a bag.

Where the change came was in successive thwack, thwack, thwacks of cool reason. With science explaining all, the supernatural world was cut away. The raisins looked around and saw the dough sheet had lifted and was now hovering several inches above them. The once-connecting world was now but a parallel world, perhaps still existing somewhere, but increasingly unreachable; incommunicable to us. By the end of the seventeenth-century in England, and with some lag in America, it was so far away that all the old beliefs began to lose their imperative oomph. How could they work any more? It used to be that witches, for example, could attach up to the backdrop world, send their maliciousness travelling along through it, and be assured that it would pop out down on their selected target. But now they couldn't reach it to connect up in the first place; prosecutions for witchcraft were rejected by one tribunal after another. Magic began to seem less likely, as did fairies and pixies and cunning men; even the old stalwart of astrology began to be turned out of respectable homes: with the upper heavens now part of nature, they could no longer be a place where pervasive sway over us could exist, to plummet earthward and control us at selected points. The once-mighty trade in sigils, those metal talismans which had been used to scoop up the astrological force as it fell from the Beyond and to hold and contain it in concentrated form to be re-used later, began to falter from lack of interest. Usury too was finally made legal, for now there was no one up there we could reach whose rightful place it was taking.

This floating away of the backdrop world, what in religious terms is the separation of man's world from God's world, suggests incidentally an answer to that question of which cause – philosophy or economics – was prior in the seventeenth-century change. The problem only makes sense if philosophy and economic doings are thought to be two very different things. (If they were similar, they wouldn't be mutually exclusive.) But that assumed difference is just the legacy of this new period, where philosophy came to be put up in That world, with God and the other Beyonds, while economics was left down in This one, a matter solely of the doings of man. No wonder researchers have had such a hard time of it. They have been trying to bridge the seventeenth-century split by using terms, from that period, which presuppose in their phrasing the very split they are trying to explain! A more prosaic approach, sticking just to the sub-lunar realm of man, seeing what can be picked up from poking around down here, might be recommended instead.

Peeling away the supernatural left even the solid material world down below different from what it had been. Gaps started opening. Where, for one, was Hell? In the sixteenth century it was a physical place, big chambers or caverns filled with brimstone and devils and people having a very bad time of it. One could imagine slipping down the right pothole and plopping, uninvited, among them. By the later seventeenth century, however, hardly any intellectuals could be found to say so any longer: Hell was interpreted as but a state of mind, the sort of place a disgruntled Virginia Woolf might say she had been when arriving late for a dinner party; it was not a physical place. (Stashing the full panoply of Hell – the demons, the absolute necessity pulling you once within it, the way it reaches out when your guilt or that of your loved ones has been especially strong – into a place called the Unconscious has been a popular salvaging operation in this century.)

Gaps also started opening up between people. In this old system there had been something called the Beggar's Curse, which intelligent, sensible people knew to watch out for. This was the imprecation any beggar could call down on you if you refused to give him some change. It worked because of the same linking up that made witchcraft work: the beggar's cries would be heard by God, travel along the backdrop thing, and re-emerge where you were, to take the proper vengeance. Without that chance of the beggar hooking up to the Beyond, though, the whole worry conveniently drops. No longer did you have to pay attention to the most insignificant of men – a poor beggar – and such paltry transactions as the passing or not of an insignificant penny. Unless you chose to feel an obligation, no-Thing else was going to grab down and make you feel it. What you didn't see, hadn't personally agreed to, went blank. It is what holding stock in a company means.

For the same reason oaths came to be increasingly replaced by promises. There's a big difference. For oaths to work you have to believe that some background thing is taking note. Even if you don't say anything you'll still feel a bit guilty if you don't do what you're supposed to; if you do go ahead and declare an oath the effect is double-strong, like sending up flares so that God, who might otherwise be distracted, can watch what you say next and be ready to zap you in the future if you don't hold to it. The replacement by promises shows that such flares were thought to go up to an empty sky. The choice of a promise instead of an oath fits in a world where I exist, and you exist, and what we do about it is up to the two of us alone:

1 January 1662: Waking this morning out of my sleep on a sudden, I did with my elbow hit my wife with a great blow over her face and nose, which waked her with pain – at which I am sorry. And to sleep again.

Had Pepys not scribbled it down later in that new-fangled, event-grasping 'shorthand', the elbow smack would have been sucked out of existence, lost forever.

It is a world where men are now separated items; the bare atoms we met earlier. Total disappearance was now a plausible concept. (Even in Hell something of you had remained.) Mathematically this was the period where there was an increased interest in negative numbers; also the first notions of a purely empty mathematical space. Both were more abstract than anything the Greeks had, and a neat match to the new abstraction of paper currency, which stayed up in a flurry of purely human creations – inked scribbles on paper – and never touched down, as metal coins did, into the solid, weighted world. The fact that there was still some invisible gooey interconnection – the new laws of physics – did not help. In theory those laws could some day be worked out in detail for men. But for the time being all they could be shown to apply to were things. The word 'coincidence' began to be used, referring to the 'juxtaposition of causally unrelated things'. The implication was that the things might just as well have not ended up juxtaposed. Where they missed, where they didn't overlap, there would be a sort of undetermined, free space. People could hunker down in that gap without anyone feeling that they were missing.

Some of the consequences were humane. Before this period ministers who guessed wrong in the governmental game usually had to be tortured, hung on the gallows, hacked into little bits, and generally made a mess of. Even if they said that frankly they preferred not to be hacked apart and that they promised very very sincerely to keep their mouths shut in the future, it was no good. All human doings being connected by that assumed background thing, their continued existence, even if they did keep quiet, couldn't be allowed. By the end of the seventeenth century, though, deposed government ministers increasingly had a more attractive fate. They could, after promising to remain quiet, be allowed to retire to a house in the country. Being an atom, in a world of separated atoms, if the ex-minister didn't say anything that really did mean he wasn't going to wend his way over to the Court and bother anyone or energize discontented factions.

Some of the consequences were less humane, however. Around those gaps in human causality, enterprising human atoms could form. Then they could stuff what they wanted inside. For the workers or other non-powerful economic agents unfortunate enough to get in their grasp, this would not be fun. Once stuffed in they were sequestered away in the strongest possible way: the metaphysics ruling the universe made their trap invisible. The men straddling the gap – paying the wages, running the joint stock companies, maybe even bossing the family – could see inside. But nobody else would even want to look. Why should they? The creation of shrouded gaps was only what the new metaphysics said was right.

It was not the worst system of all time – the previous ones had been pretty bad, with no space for anyone's personal liberty, even gap straddlers – but is, I think, the explanation of the particular bourgeois inner invisibility which we have so much of today. It's what gives management its right to manage. It's what makes the extraction of income or corporate taxes by the government such an intrusion. And it is concentrated in the concept of wages. Neither part came first. Some aspects of the time we select out and categorize as philosophy, others we select out and decide to call economic life. They combined in a certain way which makes sense, but they might have combined in some other way and made a different sense. Let us just say, in homage to the times, that what actually appeared was only one of many possible worlds. To us, looking back, it will seem a necessary one. But that's just because the possible world we happen to be in today is one of its descendants.

Before returning, finally, to our own times, a look at just one more sort of man; one regularly overlooked in the histories, and indeed overlooked in life; a quiet, generally meek creature, whose job has been described as suitable for those who find accounting too exciting; but yet a man perhaps more typical of the seventeenth-century transformations than the Sun King, or Newton, or the greatest of millionaire traders. This humble creature is the actuary. His job was to consider a man's life, use the rational science of statistics to determine its limits, and then translate that life-calculation into the monetary terms of the annuity price an insurance policy would cost. In his vision life, science and money were made as one. No one had been able to do it before. No one would have thought to do it so exactly before. Yet from the mid seventeenth century there were repeated attempts at these calculations, and by 1693 a good actuarial table was finally computed, and the profession could properly begin.

And the individual who made that first accurate, science-money-life linking table? It was none other than Edmond Halley. He was the one who just a few years before had first shown that even the great comets, which previous thinkers had been convinced arrived without rational cause and revealed a way astrology could carry out its effects on us; that these comets existed not in the atmosphere, but up in space. This showed that the cosmic realm, the assumed setting for the all-controlling Backdrop world, was too far away from us to touch. Worse, Halley even showed that the comets, including the one named in his honor, scurried around up there in accord with the simple laws of science – which meant that even the *real* Up There could not be where the Backdrop linkage occurred. In other words, there was no place left for it at all. All that was left was man, and his impersonal science – and, as Halley-when-he-slipped-on-his-new-actuary-cap showed, money: the perfect item to encapsulate the meaning of modernity's new, all-alone human creature.

V.   Emerge from the ascent of history on to the sale floor of any large department store today, and the credit cards glinting in dozens of keen shoppers' hands reveal themselves as strangely mutated successors to all that has come before. At the moment of use, as the shopper hands them over with his desired purchases, they seem to encapsulate the independence of a bourgeois world Descartes or Marx would have understood: they make the user into an autonomous being, a chevalier of finance and consumption. He wills, extends the card which is his personal identity, and he automatically becomes larger, the desired object no longer lolling out there but now part of him. But once the attendant has received the glinting credit card (or cheque) everything strangely begins to change. The shopper having handed it over becomes no longer a proud, autonomous being standing there, but instead transforms into the merest shlumping prole, every detail of his life open to inspection and viewing as the attendant feeds his card into the system that will know his credit rating and his expenditure rate and his home address and the time since his last purchase; every action he then makes dependent on the giant metal-hard system, hovering out there, of omnipotent clearing houses and banks and credit files.

In the first incarnation the credit card seems to be a tunnel to a great mirrored background that reveals to the user when he glances down onto it only a gallant image of himself, his personal intention and will. But in the second incarnation the mirrored image at the end of the tunnel begins to go misty and waver until it comes back to a new sharp focus revealing the little plastic card for what it really is: looking down onto it the user follows the tunnelway to see a powerful and unyielding clanking metal business world there at the end of it. The observant reader will see the Two Cities from the *New York Times* chapter surfacing here.

This system of monetary credit, which allows us to feel exuberantly free within the necessary acceptance of a background business system, seems to have arisen along with the growth of more fairly distributed wealth in Western countries in the years since the Second World War. The immensely larger middle class so produced could not have the true independence of the previous middle ones – with such numbers on the loose the disorder in society would be too much – but then again they wouldn't accept being explicitly pushed into a rule-following, fully constrained and bossed-about existence, as their wage-earning predecessors had. Credit cards and the credit card world handle the compromise nicely. Again it was not the only possible system, but just the one we have landed in. The freedom so produced is not absolute or even very large, but neither is it illusory – to think so is a mistake that only critics who have little experience of being on the receiving end of the factory wage-earning system are likely to make. The feeling is rather like standing under a very large machine, which has rows and rows of little toggle switches extending from its underbelly. The machine is the corporate world that envelops us; the toggles are the cheques and credit cards we can twiddle to get from it some of the things we want. More wealth has meant more toggles, and more people being given the chance to twiddle them: a hi-tech Romulus and Remus. Again it is society as a user-friendly computer: an apt label as might be expected, since it was within this society that such computers were developed and given that matching form.

The consequences of this curious way of living are many. First is that the sources that offer the items are not open to questioning. They provide, and how they do it just isn't important to us. It might be sweated labor backed by union-busting police in South Korea or Hong Kong. But where in using the system are we going to see that? The flux, with all its horrors, its uncertainties, in controlled far away from us.

Then, standing there under the machine, reaching up to get the spigot with which we hook up to it to gush, we are necessarily reaching up and twiddling alone. There is no particular reason to care for those people standing next to you reaching up to get their spigots working: you might, or you might not, but the act of using the personalized credit card does not encourage it. What it does do is encourage you to think of yourself as quite capable of surviving alone; of there being a Thing, out there, which can provide all the nourishment you need given that you attach up to it in the right way, but which no one else can help you in contacting. What is there for him to do? Help you with your signature? A stranger or even another family member who grabbed on to your arm to help you write your signature better at the cash desk would not be likely to receive a smile of thanks. Nor could he jump in earlier and try to help you with that initial volition, that individual choice of what you want. Have a kibitzer give you advice on what you wish and it is no longer your wish. Advice is only allowed from official advertisers or personnel specialized in selling your desired goods, and those are creatures who are not really down in this world, worrisome fellow creatures next to you, but are rather emissaries, ethereal barely existent emanations of that higher world up there, which is the business system that you are aiming to extract a part from anyway. What happens to the eager financial services salesperson beckoning to you from behind the counter at Sears? He has in his job no personality or troubling individual existence. Come five o'clock he disappears from the earthly vale; only the company behind him, eternal, will remain.

It is not unique to our times to believe that there is a supporting backdrop realm, towards which we just have to select the right spot to hook up to and we will be okay. Religion has had something to say on this subject for a long time. God is the eternally existing power back there, and individual or priest-assisted prayer is the way to hook up and get the desired spiritual nourishment. It's a safe way to touch the powers *mysticum*. Even for the requirements of economic man something like it has been around long before the era of credit cards.

The feeling with early joint-stock companies was that they were places where the source of all power circulated, into which we could reach, pull out paper credits, and materialize them into useful goodies. With paid jobs in general the feeling is still that there's a flow of money out there, with individual slots for us, and that by being hired we plug in to get some of it. The change, with credit cards, is only a matter of nuance. But such an important one. The hooking up now requires much less visible co-operation; it accordingly is one where the Other Side seems to prove itself to each and every one of us separately. Credit cards are not the underlying cause of the current attitudes, but nor are they simply a consequence. They are the sticky bits in between – what David Hume left out. Logically there's no need for them. But practically they, with their requirements of a flourished individual signature, are the medium through which today's system speaks to us. The average American or Briton makes a tremendous number of credit card or check transactions each week. And such repeated practices can only leave one habituated to the pattern they take.

For the family, this has not been good. Everybody can take care of themselves, or so the system encourages one to think, and so anyone to whom you do not feel impelled to croon

Amo, amas, I love a lass,

or even whom you are just temporarily bored with, can be dropped at will. Husbands shed wives, wives shed husbands, and post-adolescent children try to shed both parents. It is an odd and recent quirk. In the 1930s it would have been cruel for a husband to dump his wife, and unwise for a child to try to flee his parents. A denuded creature could starve. There was too little assured wealth. Bonds with family were crucial. This is not so now. Individuals who lived through the Depression generally have a strong awareness of kinship terms. Their children and grand-children, however, are frequently embarrassed by the careful recital of just which second cousin that individual kibitzing at the wedding or funeral is. It is a bond that nothing in current economics encourages one to pay attention to. What has the second cousin ever done for me? That utilitarian question is a mischevous one, and if continued will end with spouses and parents failing too.

The result is separated atoms, but not as it turns out very private ones. Privacy means doing things without other people knowing.

But it's not possible to use a credit card without lots of people knowing what you want, and indeed knowing exactly where you are. Imagine Sky Masterson calling a pause just before his final craps shot to have Nicely-Nicely carry up to police HQ a statement of where the game is taking place. The commissioner would think it was a hoax. In our case the triplicate flimsies that come with credit card dealings do as much, and the clearing houses and banks take it as their due.

Once our location is given, once we do plug in to the enveloping system, we can't stop what's up there from pouring in. There are no convenient gaps in causality within which to shelter and watch the outer torrent pass. How could there be? Switch on a television or compact disc and you have created a personal space around you, but it is not a private one. Everyone if they wish can see what is on television, or listen to the current compact disc offerings. Similarly for your trying to hunker down inside current clothing fashions, cars, new furniture and most books. Other people can peer inside them too. All is open to inspection, fairly enough, since all are just various manifestations of the large Backdrop Thing. It talks, and we listen. Sitting in a room *mano a mano* with a television set, nothing you do, no glares or winks or even hands-clasped passionate implorement, will get it to change what it has to offer. Flick the channel, or switch on a video from the local shop, and there is only a little improvement. There is still no creativity, since choice is still restricted to a selection among the pre-given. The hierarchical mimicking is again delightful. All that the toggle switches of individual purchasing have produced are items that themselves offer but toggle switches to fullfil individual urge.

Even the naked body has to succumb. When Baden-Powell went out striding for his morning constitutional, if he came to a little hill and got tired he would apply a little willpower and keep on going. If he came to a large hill and got very tired he would apply a large amount of willpower and still keep on going. This willpower was something he carried around in him in little packets somewhere in his brain or, if a great deal was called for, there were also containers of willpower which doubled as receiving stations for calling in extra supplies from the past, especially boarding school, or from distant locations in the present, such as the Queen needing protection on her throne, or the nation as a whole. It is an easy attitude to parody, since it can be so easily applied to insignificant or undesirable tasks, but it is also an important attitude, being both very widespread and also capable, at times, of producing persistence in very noble tasks. (Baden-Powell and his setting were indeed historically a source point for the modern development of commandos.)

The credit card man would not know what inner sources of willpower are. If he gets tired on a job, he should stop. It might be shin splints, or fertility impairment, or the beginning of a coronary attack. This is not paranoia. This is but common sense. The body is not to be pushed. Nothing is to be pushed. Rather the body is to be listened to, opened up and examined through a careful attention to how it feels – a little session of physiological phenomenology there on the jogging trail – and a comparison of that feeling with all the lessons remembered from science programs and running books. What sort of nut would want to skip that? He would have to be a private being, used to an autonomy that includes space for reference to a private motivator within. The paused runner, fingers on his wrist checking pulse against his digital watch, wincing as he thinks through the systems of his body and notes every twinge, might see such a creature striding up a distant hill, arms swinging and muttering about Charterhouse and Mafeking. But he himself will feel none of that.

The separate being really no longer exists. He has been allowed to be so distinct from his fellows, so used to being free-standing in his wishes and their satisfaction, that the space he takes up has in comparison with the larger Thing shrunk down, down, down: past individual, atom, or even infinitesimal, to just the point source memory of a ghost that once had been. Knowledge packs too tightly around him, since it is now, as opposed to the seventeenth-century epistemology, a knowledge designed to apply to man and all his desires. And the source of this human knowledge is now unimpeachable. Where once our existence in God's body would have held every detail, so that one couldn't hide even in the bowels of Christ, now it is the consumption offerings of the new Out There, the one the credit card reaches up to, which we accept are to reach into and indeed take over our inner spaces.

The consequence in politics is support for the conservative democracy of the sort that Reagan and Thatcher had been keen on. In those political visions every individual is infinitely free, infinitely capable of acting out their own volition, however wild or self-chosen it is; yet at the same time all individuals must also accept, will wish to accept, an immensely powerful background state, that links all, that controls all, that is the source of all. You can buy Walkmans or move away from your old neighborhood or go wild and splurge on a nice car; yet you must also accept the requirements of the City, or oil companies, or the defense department procurement system as the backdrop matrix within which you do your volitional scurryings. It is an amiable authoritarianism – and geared down an abstraction level it matches quite neatly that system of purchasing by credit card or cheques where there is both an act of pure volition (that moment of handing over the card to get what is wanted), and also an acceptance of the encompassing credit system, that certifies, ratifies, and has rules that must be obeyed. The conclusion is not that Democrats and Labour will never be let back in. In time the public comes to see the merit of throwing out any bum who has been in office too long. Also there are other, sometimes contradictory, forces in current society. But the day-to-day process of obtaining goods will not encourage sharing with all.

It is a conservatism beyond spoken language, for with words one can always create the opposite of what has been said. That has been the weakness of attempts to create an inherently anti-revolutionary language, from Hobbes on up. But credit card money is a brute thing, so we cannot escape from the single kind of dealing it demands. With some finagling you can get even a restricted vocabulary to say *MinLove Doubleplusungood* and then wonder what curious meaning it might have, but however you hold it a credit card can communicate only one thing. There will be little shared feeling for the creation or maintenance of, say, a National Health Service covering everyone. Too many people, not sharing in the credit dealings and toggle switchings, will be quite naturally left out. There is something of the traditional selfishness of money in this. But when that held the numbers on the outside were a majority. Now, in the wealthy countries, they're not. The remnant is the new underclass. The quite extraordinary viciousness of personal muggings by individuals from many American city slums is perhaps due to their responding to this treatment, which is among the most insulting of all: that of being ontologically shunned. All signs are that other countries can expect more of the same treat as they follow the American future.

And the reasons for accepting the system? The apparent ones we have already met. There is the possibility of at least some selection, which is more than most humankind has had; there is also the apparent destruction of individual boss-men, whence the pleasures in our service economy of all seeming to be serving each other – one of the nicest attractions of orthodox communism, in Reagan's America finally made true. But there is another reason, one more powerful still. The Up There which is on offer now, the one above and rewarding human dealings, is not God, as it once was, nor even physics, which it was at a later time at least for educated sub-groups. It is people, what in finance matches the large corporations whose name we see etched on our credit cards, and whose image we detect shimmering at the top of the causality funnel they open up.

This too is not, by itself, brand new. The comforts of huge population bindings through nationalism pre-date it, as the national symbols on paper money show. But those speak to all of us. They are impersonal in their targeting. Credit cards, one step up, are not. They only work if their personal operator chooses to make them work. It's like an SOE agent hunched over a crystal radio in the backroom of the French café, trying to reach London HQ through the crackle and hiss. He's the only one who can get the radio to work, so he's the only one to get to speak with London when finally the signal comes through. Similarly for the man pulling his credit card from his wallet. Here the communication being set up will punch through the static, past any earthly HQ, all the way to the Beyond. When the answer comes back he gets suffused with power. That's the pleasure of the credit card, its lovely advantage over money. Using it we become the spot where the Backdrop comes through. That is nice. That is also unique. For now, finally, with the cards, we each get the pleasure of being individually blessed.

Part Four
Consolations

It starts in comedy, with Doll Tearsheet jibing:

When wilt thou leave fighting o'days and foining o'nights, and begin to patch up thine old body for heaven?

But then there is a long, long pause, and Falstaff, no buffoon at all now, quietly replies:

Peace, good Doll! do not speak like a death's-head; do not bid me remember mine end.

Yet of course, sadly, he must remember, as must we all. The fact of our personal extinction is one we cannot ignore. All societies have to offer some solace against it. The solace doesn't have to be logical, or perfect; just persuasive. We can't really go through life otherwise.

What that solace is today, what these deepest backings for our life are, in America as well as in Europe, we will now consider.

8

A Quiet Afternoon

Observe the Englishman on a Sunday afternoon. He has his newspaper, and he wants for nothing else. There is the ritual of surrounding himself with the paper, of immersing himself in it as in a soothing hot bath, often after setting up in a soft chair, with a cup of tea at hand and obligations to other family members or friends fulfilled so that, once the read is begun, all intruders or interrupters can be ignored, perhaps scowled away, to leave the reader in his soothing peace. Sometimes the preparation even includes a quick skim of the paper first, a masochistic passing over of the delights, purely so that the best articles, 'The kind I like', can be noted and savoured for the moment of total immersion to come.

This is a very curious thing to do. Many of the people who will spend a good hour with the paper on a Sunday would never spend an hour reading one thing at any time in the week; indeed the articles they will read on the Sunday might include massive, 1,000-word features on topics such as industrial disputes, policy on Eastern Europe, and other technical, detailed matters. One thousand words of discourse on such topics from a stranger on the bus would rarely be taken to kindly. Yet here it is enjoyed. Something is going on to make the reader do this to himself now, in the privacy of his own couch. But what?

It is, of course, the consolation of practical philosophy. Reading his Sunday paper the Englishman gets to rebuild the assumptions that get terribly banged up in the rest of the week. He gets to see all his hopes and guiding actions reaffirmed: the workings of history and death, chance and money – all are set out just as he needs. It is not that he is being told what to think. The man in his soft chair, feet up and slippers on, would be too obstinate for that. Rather he is being reminded of what he already thinks, and consoled that that noble edifice is true. What we shall do is look over his shoulder, and peek at that edifice too.

But first a detail: a choice of starting points, a spot on the embarkation quay. Unlike the man in his chair, who already knows what newspaper he wants, who would grunt and harrumph from the depths of his being if the wrong one were deposited in his home by mistake, we must choose which one to peruse. Will it be the *News of the World*, with its vicars and nipples and sporting stars all tangled in a heap? Or the *Mail on Sunday*, pride of the Rothermere line? Or the *Observer, Sunday Telegraph, Sunday People* or another? All have their attractions, but for our purposes there will be no choice but the (London) *Sunday Times*. This is Britain's most respected Sunday paper: a sensible intermediary between the extremes of the *Observer* and *Sunday Telegraph*, with a huge circulation, huge advertising revenues, and a huge and still much envied staff of writers.

What is the consolation that the reclining Englishman sees in his *Sunday Times*? At first it might seem that it should be the same as what the American, lox and bagels and fresh orange juice or other treat at the ready, finds in his *Sunday New York Times*. Readers of both papers are what the advertising people call A and B people: the top, and most respectable middle, people in both countries. They have similar educations, similar sized families, similar ways of investing their money and making their money and heating their homes and buying their clothes and doing all the other things people can do that make them similar or not. And indeed both papers give facts, lots of them, as well as hints at the way those facts will work out in the future so as to let those readers assess the world and move around in it as they need. Where the difference comes is in the particular kinds of moves the different readers will wish to make. That is immensely important, for it shows what you most care for and choose. To find out what those different moves are we now need to swoop in even closer to the man with the *Sunday Times*, his gas-fired central heating on, all intruders safely away, and see how he starts his luxurious read.

What he begins with first of all is the front page. This is usual. This also is chaos. In just a few weeks in 1987 readers had to cope with the knowledge of:

CHAOS IN THE CHUNNEL

ZIRCON SECRET THAT COULDN'T BE KEPT

MP GO-BETWEEN IN MI5 PAY-OFF

along with incidentals such as the fact that a former head of British Intelligence may have been not a loyal British civil servant but a

Soviet spy, and other matters. It is a blur, a rush, a wild gush of facts and disorientating, generally unpleasant data.

Although these are the first thing our reader turns to in his paper, it is not because he is a maniac, a fetishist, keen on purveyors of gore and surprise. He knows his paper too well for that; he knows that the page one doings will be made orderly and above all acceptable without delay. Some of the ways the paper puts him at ease with them are the same as the way the *New York Times* handles it: a bit of tabloid comforting for catastrophes such as air crashes; more restrained terrain assessment surveys for the rest. Yet also with the *Sunday Times* there is another way of handling these strange intrusions. This is to let them happen, to dwell and revel in their coarse irruptions and then, just when they're getting really bad, to get the reader to think very hard about something else, something cool and orderly and soothing and nice. Have him do this hard enough and he will be transported from the realm of bad to a realm of good; from the chaos and pay-offs and spies around him to a heaven as beautiful as only he can imagine.

The reader does not need to close his eyes and scrunch his face and maybe tap his heels together like Dorothy had to when she and Toto wanted to get back to home in Kansas to achieve this. All he has to do is poke around in the stack of the paper until he comes up with the Magazine section, and then turn to its back page. There he will find exactly that soothing vision he needs: one where the world is not chaotic, but in harmony; where all that is bad has been banished, and only what is good can be found. This vision is the regular 'Life in the Day of' feature, which informal surveys show is one of the most likely places for buyers to turn after a quick skim of the news. It is a full-page account, with photograph, of a typical day in the life of some person, generally famous or unusual (a Lord, a TV star), but sometimes ordinary (a housewife, a traffic policeman). Here is something that if landed in the *New York Times* would shock the American reader, perhaps enough to have him sit up on his couch, spilling the orange juice in alarm. In the *New York Times* a life being described would show coping, improvisation, an emphasis on the new and unsure. In the London *Sunday Times*, though, it is a page with a vision that is almost Un-American: the reporters are instructed to bring out from the subjects, often famous and so apparently emulable, details showing that what they do in their life is nothing but repeat what they have done before. Nothing fresh, disturbing, or strange is allowed to occur there. The subjects get up, see the same

people, fit their impulses into the same pre-set arrangements, and then
end the day and go to sleep, in the same way as they have every other
day. The 'Life in the Day of' subjects have everything worked out
and made stable and controlled. They would not have been invited in
otherwise.

   The rest of the paper, the matter of all the bumf in between, can be
seen as largely a way of giving the chair-recumbent reader enough
pointers to make the progression from chaos to order himself. It is a
difficult task, but the London *Sunday Times* is a thick paper. Christian
on his difficult way to heaven could not have had more object lessons.
There are ogres and false lures, shimmering visions and voices of wise
counsel. All the *Sunday Times* reader has to do is interpret them
appropriately, which is why he struggles, why he concentrates and
demands silence, while he reads.

   Not every English Sunday paper reader has such a hard task. For
Sunday Telegraph readers the job of interpreting their own newspaper
is a breeze. *Telegraph* readers see a chaotic world, they're offered the
vision of tranquility through eternal repetition, too, but the way
they're told to join that vision is simply to hide themselves away from
the world. This is clear from the standard *Telegraph* anger article, the
one where a heroic but now poor pensioner is attacked by a young
black mugger. The pensioner should have invested in an insurance
society or other sure thing so that he would have enough money for a
more protected home, or to live in a better protected neighborhood;
on a larger scale there should be enough police and harsh judges
around to form an outer perimeter to keep mugging dangers from
ever getting to our homes, our lives. It is what might be called the
retrenching solution, which is why the *Sunday Telegraph* conveniently offers its tremendous number of sure-fire investment ads, as well
as indignant editorial objections to those who would hamper the
police or tamper with society in ways that would let any new thing
in.

   Unfortunately *Sunday Times* readers are not content to be
instructed on how to hide away from the world. They're not ready to
settle for what they have yet. The *Sunday Times*'s tension is that while
it is ultimately teaching people to prepare a defense against the chaotic
world, it also needs to show them, American style, how to analyze the
world and move along in it. It is neither fully one nor the other. The
result is an attitude of tentative forays, of peeking out to accumulate
information about the outside from the shelter of a good cocoon and
then, when all is ready, rushing out to make your move before

rushing back in again, hopefully in a higher or broader or better connected niche.

This makes for some odd distortions. Because it has to be left for these terrifying forays, the cocoon the *Sunday Times* reader lives in between-times cannot be your basic gate-off-the-world cocoon, a simply health-insured, mortgaged and double-glazed blockade, but rather must be an open cocoon, a moving cocoon, a cocoon that by the very process of being in it gets the reader used to sailing in the open world. Nor, however, can it be in full contact with that outside world. There is a curious sense of holding back. The compromise result is the BMW to look out of, the modemed computer to nourish from, and even the thrilling experience of going to new ethnic restaurants, where although the visitor is cocooned in the structure of going to a restaurant, with all the defenses of servility and order and defined choice that means, he still gets to experience strange things of the outside world being incredibly close, all around him, spurting in via the menu and decor and alien people who in this setting he lets almost touch him. The *Sunday Telegraph* reader at the retrenching extreme, glaring out from his double-glazed patio, clutching his medical insurance protection from hernia and goiter and unmentionable intestinal complaints, will never get this exciting knowledge to use. The *New York Times* reader at the other extreme, taking it for granted that he should be regularly dealing with the world, will use it all the time without unease. It is only the *Sunday Times* man who is stuck, socially exhausted, in between.

Why does he suffer so? The problem is that the *Sunday Times* reader is trying to do an American thing in an English setting. He is trying to get ahead, to assess the world and move along in it, but he is trying to do this not for the sake of the voyage, but for the sake of ending up in a passive, locked-in, guaranteed state of being at the end. At heart it is a difference in the standards of what is most important, especially in the solutions to the problem of death which every society has to come up with. Americans tend, as has been noted, to have what might be called a Tarzan theory of immortality, where their only chance of survival is to try to share in the future, which means they will grab on to any dangling ropes of it – any examples of the newest and the latest – that happen to stretch backwards into the present where they now live. It is like Tarzan leaping for a vine. This can unite large numbers of people, because they are all striving in the same direction, even if, being in the future and so still unclear, it provides few detailed standards on how to act now.

In Europe generally and in Britain, or rather in traditional Britain, the underlying consolation against death has been different. There has come to be instead what could be called the Time Capsule theory of immortality, where the way one manages to survive is by encapsulating oneself in a guaranteed and fully contained setting which will then, by sheer inertia, carry on into the future. That setting will largely be built up of habitual social relations, backed by guaranteed sources for money. This was the natural solution for an aristocracy to develop for themselves – their families and the family income are quite visibly what get passed on – and also is something that individuals at any detailed slot in the class system could be comforted by – a neat double-working good for social harmony too. In both the American and British cases, although literal personal immortality cannot be assured – that is too much to ask – these solutions will do as ways of getting out of the horrid flux of time.

Since the *Sunday Times* man is in between, the revised image we get for his setting shows a whole flotilla of little spheres bobbing on a stormy river. The spheres are the various British time capsules of particular class setting; the river moving forward is the flux of time. Everyone is hunched down inside their particular capsule like little leprechauns . . . except for the poor *Sunday Times* man, who is not content with the one he has been landed in, and has to crack open the door, peer around outside amidst the rain and waves, and then somehow clamber or leap from his original capsule to the target one he has in mind. Once he has made it he can crawl in, pull the hatch closed behind him, and hope he'll be allowed to join the others there. But until then he has to suffer. This is the curious task his newspaper supports him in, by its shape of moving from a chaotic page one, where the howling and rain pour in, all the way to the harmonious 'Day in the Life of' feature, waiting warm and inviting there at the end.

This struggle for advancement into stasis, vicariously lived through by the reader with feet up by the fire, is interesting not just for what it can reveal about Britain today, but also because it is a problem which all of us in late-industrial Western countries suffer from. There is the attraction of the past, the attraction of the future – and we are never content with just one. Consider life within one of those bobbing, self-maintaining spheres. Is this not a dream we all have, to be cosseted, loved, taken care of? It is the hearth, family, mother, support; the most satisfying part of the old 'pulling into the familiar' tabloid attitude. But then take life on the outside of one of those capsules, struggling in the rain and waves with a leap ahead. This too is attractive: it is the eternal dream of exploring, adventuring, and escape; of voyaging forth and blazing trails and generally having a hell of a time in the process; the soaring flights of the assessing conditional in operation.

This is what makes the *Sunday Times* so important. The approaches to secular immortality described above are logically distinct, but in fact will often be merged. So will the different choices of harmony or adventure they presuppose. Our personalities, our ideals demand it. It would be a poor simplification to say that the English always take the settled choice, Americans the adventuruous. At different points in European history almost every country – Italy, Flanders, France, England, Germany – has been held out as having citizens obsessed with ceaseless and blind future-loving action. Only ideal types are that simple, not real people. What we shall be able to see in the *Sunday Times* are a group of people – the English middle classes – who are exquisitely stretched between these two poles. Their struggles will illuminate the world of us all.

II. The first ideal, that of being cosseted and warm, is best illustrated in the English aristocracy. To understand these individuals we could do worse than to start with the horses they are so often photographed with. Both mammals in such pictures are there only because the attributes they have are ones that can be guaranteed, pre-set, before birth. This is why you do not see photographs in the *Sunday Times* of aristocrats with slide rules, or adjusting a bunsen burner. Intelligence is not something that can be guaranteed. You could not imagine Lady Di or her friends running a home for gifted youngsters. The comparison with their charges would be disheartening. But you could imagine them, with delight and a sense of deep self-fulfilment, running a stable. A horse, genetically, will weigh a ton and have long legs and be capable of running fast. That is assured. Volition, and the quirks of individual horse-hood, do not enter into it. The aristocrats, though beasts of a lesser weight, are also in a setting that is fully assured, independent of their whims or strengths, within which they need not struggle to get along. All they need to do is be.

This assured setting, where a continued existence as you wish comes automatically, is of course a transposition of the religious concept of heaven. The analogy is close, because the reasoning is close. The world of sense and change around us is an exhausting, generally terrifying thing. The idea of a break-out, of an escape to a realm where all is certain and, best of all, we never have to work again, is a continual temptation. For most of us it will only happen with death, but some are lucky and get there before. They might have to move slowly, statically, as if to emphasize that they're half-dead, but that's not hard for the rewards they get.

With these happy escapers having such a good time, the question becomes how to get what they have, or at least a bit more of it. Murder followed by theft is tempting, but produces legal problems. Concentration on sweaty biological couplings is another possible solution, a capacity even the tabloid readers have in common with the top people, and so the grounds for all those stories on Sex Craving Royals and Over-Heated Rich Girls. But that too is of little practicable use. It is only the approach the *Sunday Times* takes which offers a useful way in. What exactly *is* that effortless glide the aristocracy get to go through? It is composed of two things. First, there are the right rules of social behaviour, so that the aristocrats don't have to worry about how to act towards any possible person they come across, choice and uncertainty eliminated. Then there is the backdrop supporting structure of money, lots of it, so much and so well ensconced in things like land or property or investments which produce more of the lovely stuff without the owner ever having to worry about it, that it can provide the aristocrats with all the items they need to carry out the ideal rules of social behaviour they know. For the practical emulator, then, the task will be uncovering right behaviour, and uncovering sources of the right sort of money – exactly the subjects for which the *Sunday Times* offers itself as the indispensable guide. It won't touch on the actual objects the aristocracy are concerned with – it will be all middle-class and upper-middle-class goodies and sources of wealth instead – but the template, the image being matched, will be from on high.

Such mimicking of action on one level from a model on another, what might seem to be totally disparate level is surprisingly common. Sometimes it will go from a microcosm out, as, for example, with conservative papers yanking their view of small neighborhood doings into their reporting of foreign affairs. That young black mugger attacking an elderly veteran is quite neatly the country as a whole, noble from its action in the past or in past wars but now sadly decayed, being assaulted by change and external, foreign influences. Sometimes the mimicry goes the other way, from macrocosm in. Thus in TV game-shows the contestant is presented with a world that is smaller than the real world – just the size of a studio sound stage in fact – and has on it struggles which correspond to the contests of real life, but again similarly reduced, so that they become a small contest with a machine, or a questioning host, or some other single event where the rules are more easily specified and understood than outside.

This is what the *Sunday Times* readers are doing with the aristocracy. They want the stasis ideal, and with the aristocracy around to copy it from that's where they will turn to pick out the techniques. It is a natural choice. It is also a useful one. For if there are to be capsules of social behavior, why shouldn't they be ranked in a row, with one lucky capsule officially getting to live it up at the front?

To some extent this has been automatic, a consequence of the fact that, as Aquinas noted, serial ranking is one of the easiest ways to put form upon diversity. To some extent it has been thought out, though; a reification of the order to stay in your place, which betters in the political system have always realized was a convenient rule to get everyone else to fall for. It was made especially rigid in England by having been introduced with early industrialism, on the ground floor as it were. That was order not just for serfs or the mob, but for those with all the fine range of jobs in industrial society – what has continued, roughly, till now. So long as there was no revolution, this would have to be the alternative. It's fitting that polite queueing, that popular activity foreigners now remark upon with anthropological delight, seems also to have got going in Britain around the middle of the last century, when the revolutionary solution had been definitely stopped. Before then visitors to Britain often remarked on how pushy, elbow-bashing, and emotional its crowds were.

Given the ranking, there are also reasons other than pure chance that the people lower down would pick out social relations to mimic that were assured and repeating, like those of the aristocrats. Concern with right behaviour is natural to all humans as social creatures, and when there is that Time Capsule theory of immortality around telling us that what we do automatically – have friends, have children with the right sort of friends – can be our salvation, then we'll be especially primed to study the right way to act and consider interconnection with others as our way to the Beyond. Also once the Time Capsule theory began, that would knock other of the logical possibilities of secular salvation aside, at least for a while. Most Europeans, in the past few centuries, have just continued to live in that while.

There are also good reasons why the majority should have picked out the monetary backing of the aristocracy as crucial. All of us know how we can put ourselves in a warm bubble of assurance and ease in the moment of purchasing something with money. For a brief moment the thing you want is yours, and all your bidding will be done. (In excess this is the practice of going to a restaurant for the sake of ordering the waiters around, a practice apparently immensely satisfying to the doers, as all who have observed it can testify.) How much more wonderful it would be to have this all the time. The important point is not that money is needed for a good life. This no one needs the particular model of an aristocracy to tell them. Rather it's that to get the general supporting we want, money will have to be there, but held in the backdrop: it will have to be invisible ectoplasmic money, which is behind us, and around us, and holding us up, but never ever there to be seen. This is the key. Show the money even once, and the free ride would be gone.

It is a difficult task and there are a lot of people who fail at it. Many Americans especially shatter the mood of the seance by blurting out on the slightest incentive, or even just at a lull in the conversation, statements of what they earn, how they earn it, and then, for good measure and out of a sense of fairness, questions about just what is it that the Englishman they're talking to – now perhaps going white and trying to back away – himself earns. This is no good. This is not what a person should do. Maybe it's okay if you believe that life is redeemed by surging towards the future, with money just one of the tools to help give you a leg up, but that's not the general English belief. Where is the harmony in that, the buddy-buddiness, shared friendliness, and relief at eternally unchanged links with those around you? It is gone. The blurting is not just gauche, but a personal insult, a thwarting, to those who see salvation this other way.

The proper method is to use indirect cues. The Englishman will not ask his host how much he earns. What he will do is note, with exquisite care, every surface sign he can get of what his host earns, or even better, as earning itself might be too coarse or active, every sign of what money his host has access to. Is he in a guaranteed niche, and how does it compare to yours? It is not just a matter of being attentive to the indirect social signs of your host's level in society, the he-had-the-Mahler-tape-just-started-when-we-came-in-so-he-must-be-keen-to-show-us-he's-one-above-the-Tchaikovsky-listener's-level sort of reasoning. That everybody does. Humans can't help picking up such friendship or hostility markers. It's something of a reflex. What's special is the extraordinary attempt to pick out anything that has to do with money, while the host, despite knowing how important this is, has to do his best to hide that backing. As an added complication the host will be picking apart the guest as soon as he leaves just as much as the guest, once in his car, will be steeling his eyes and commenting with hate ('stretching his means a bit, don't you think?') or reverence ('he's doing *quite* well, I would think') on the true financial supports of the host. It is a smiling, slow-motion war, which both sides must demonstrate to have won without trying. There is a desire, a mutual desperation, to make sure that all the meanings of any possible financial referent are picked up in exactly the right way: a search for the right word, right tone, right response, to every possible spoken or physical gambit that might be tried.

The experience is exhausting, and produces a certain brittleness of personality. It will not be limited to UK citizens, but will be evident in anyone who accepts the blissful invisible time capsule as the goal. Certain Americans have even been reported as acting this way.

So much for the first pull of attraction, that of being cossetted and warm, life inside the protective spheres. Now for the other one: the emergence out of an all-embracing sphere, and the indelicate scrambling in the outside world. Why do we do it? The answer, almost always, is because the warm, cossetted, etc. realm we started with is not good enough. For four or five generations now – about a century or more, depending on the place – Western nations have been getting richer, fast. This has brought almost every family into a new, generally more comfortable setting. That improvement entered the world of assumed ideas, and resulted in a tremendously widespread personal belief in the old Whig interpretation of history: not theoretical, not dependent on a reading of Macaulay, or a checking of footnotes in Butterfield, but practical, lived out, from the actual experience of life having become steadily easier. It is the belief by individuals that they can improve just as their country as a whole has.

This spattering of the overall progress belief on to each individual is essential. Without it we would have a country getting richer and stronger but everyone in it holding to their previous position. This is the old conservative fantasy of one's own nation as a great armored battleship, hatches closed and all guns firing, steaming on in harmony into the future. It's an idea that gets support from the tabloid attitude of wanting only the familiar, as also from all our desires for a warm capsule, but founders on the point that while it's great if you happen to be the captain, it's less great if you're one of the coal shovellers. Charters and Caldicott were in that ship, travelling protected by their standards in a foreign land, but who would want to be the servant shlepping their bags? What makes the official American attitude so attractive is that it gets around that limitation, and speaks to each and every one of us, offering to all the promise of relative advance as great as that of the whole country. Does the nation leap-frog through time? Then we shall leap-frog our position within it too.

These reasons for escaping the capsule we happen to be landed in are so strong that they can get inside the body of the person so liberated and make him, zombie-like, wish to stretch out his arms and do things that in his wiser moments he would never consider. Take that feeling of individual improvement since the time of our ancestors only a few generations back. Almost every reader of the *Sunday Times* had great-great grandparents who were so poor and miserable that it would be excruciating if through some strange warp in time they were to be beamed forward and plopped into the reader's home today. Think of their eating habits. Think of the vermin and miserable clothes and lack of knowledge and their attitudes of subservience; think of the accent! It would horrify the children, looking up from their home computer, and it would embarrass, it would disgrace, the parent.

The reader knows this, knows that almost all that's good about him is due to his being a creature of the present and that oh-so-recent upswing that produced it, and will wish to do the opposite of dwell on his ancestors beyond the level of grandparents or so. The past, the imtimate flesh-of-thine-flesh past, is something horrid, a family secret, to be locked in an upstairs storeroom and kept there, not even the corridor that passes near it to be travelled along with ease. Older people alive today who are befuddled at why the progeny who they've always tried to be nice to now shun them, act almost embarrassed by them, are just on the receiving end of this fear.

It is an unkind thing to do, but the economically successful society demands it. And, fair is fair, that society gives to all but these old people something back in return. It gives the new, it gives the present, it gives items that are not aged or rusty or wrinkled or anything other than sparkling and fresh. That is something very many people want, desperately. Although the fact is that we all have the same biological rootedness in the past – eight great-grandparents, several hundred or more at the tenth generation back – with such items of the new on offer we can be free of that. Anything that confirms the virtues of newness will accordingly be reached for, grabbed, gathered in without discretion, for the solace, the assertion of independence from the wrong kind of history, our personal secret history, that it provides. That is the lure of wine-bars and slick new restaurants generally. That is why *Sunday Times* readers will rarely be content to read just the fact-loaded features in the color magazine supplement that comes with their paper. That supplement will have to be leafed through comprehensively, so that all the glossy ads can be noted too. It might be a flick, a quick REMed dash from page to page while the spouse stands there fuming, waiting for her magazine, but it will almost always be done. Clothes, cars, cigarettes, furniture, lawnmowers, cameras, perfume and most of the other goodies for sale there are inherently 'just made'. They are another thing with shallow roots. By analogy they become the reader, and by choosing and valuing them what he's doing is choosing and valuing himself. Plucking them from the firmament, even in imagination, he becomes girded with a shield against the past and its slurping, hideous hold.

Dislike of ancestors also helps explain, I suspect, the bizarre thing a *Sunday Times* reader is supposed to get up to when he goes to France. What, in the words of his magazine and newspaper articles, constitutes a successful trip there? Good restaurants, of course, good hotel rooms and weather, but also, mixed in with all that, something they would never wish to do at home: a meaningful relationship with a French peasant. The reader is supposed to meet him, at a charming village café perhaps; listen to his opinions, nod with a delightful smile while he purses his lips and fondles his beret before going on with another opinion, and then, who knows, if luck and the fates are right, perhaps even get to be invited back to his home for a meal.

This is odd for anyone, but especially for a middle-class Englishman. He is unlikely to travel around his own country, sidling up to rural labourers or workers in pubs, starting up a conversation, smiling with delight at any comment elicited, and hoping against hope to be invited back home for some bangers and mash. It is not the done thing. But on a trip to France, it is *de rigueur*. Whatever could the reason be?

Think again who that French peasant is. He is an older man, a sign of something that has not changed much over time, a living remnant of the past . . . and yet he is not horrible, repulsive, terrible to have around. Rather he is wonderful. He can speak French for one; he can blend in at a French café, he can cook food better than anything you'll find in the supermarket, he knows about wine, he has no complexes about mistresses; in short he does things the upper class would be desperate to be able to do themselves, and he does it perfectly, by his nature, without any worry. This is a miracle. He is a sign of what the

Englishman could have been, without any effort, if only his damned ancestors had had the good sense to be poor peasants in France instead of at home. He would, automatically, and just by continuing true to what he had been, be in a life that the English aristocracy would wish to emulate. He would be flying! One counterfactual is all it would have needed. It is no surprise, then, that the English middle classes are so keen to observe, to meet, to get as close as possible to that French peasant: it is a way of paying homage to a favored, and alternate, self.

Alternate 'selves' at home are not so desirable. They're too close. Even if the relation is not certain, even if no 'Ah, how the unpleasant mannerisms of great-great-great- . . . great Aunty Brunhilde the *villein* come out in that coarse man by the cigarette machine' springs to mind, there's still a deep feeling that all Englishmen came from the same roots, the same country. It's too mingled a population pool. Let the *Sunday Times* reader be forced to wait at Dover station next to a countryman who doesn't have exactly his own surface manners, and the past of muck-trudging serfhood that countryman is revealing in his actions will be a distorted, unpleasant image of what is there inside the travelling reader too; whence the revulsion, distancing and horror usual in such encounters. White Americans are less likely to be so horrified by each other, for they know they come from different countries — so many that no Aunty Brunhilde could straddle them all — and so are not that likely to be biologically linked, at least on the same time-scale as traditional nations. Their only historical link would have been the choice to become good Americans. If one is richer than the other he just happens to be better at doing the thing both those ancestors said they wanted. There's some room for snobbery here, but not for that hatred of the countryman's being. The politics of a Margaret Thatcher, with its distaste for anything having to do with workers (Thatcher herself having that dreaded lower-class being immersed only two generations deep within her), gets little general support in America.

Combine the two poles of attraction — the ideal of a warm, encompassing bubble, plus the ideal of scrambling from one into another — and the real catastrophes begin. However are you going to get into the new one? Those bubble cocoons are closed up, snug, without a seam. That was their whole pleasure. Where will there be the loose join, or not-quite-closed hatch, which a newcomer could use to get inside it?

It's a problem in all countries where there is social mobility, but it will be especially clear in Britain, where the topmost bubble is so clear and inviting, and yet also so old that any seams which might have opened up during its making have long since been welded over. The only solution is to fall back to the old infallible tool of ready money. It was money at a certain level that maintained the group our social voyager started from, and, as any glance into the Beyond will reveal, it is money that encompasses and supports the target group in its shimmering bubble which he has his eye on. This is the natural device to turn to: it will be the darning hook for ripping open a gap in the woven cocoons; a crowbar to clankingly lever open a riveted porthole.

But where to sink the money tool in? Money is powerful because it is a tool usable by anyone, but being so universal it carries no rule-sheet telling you exactly how to use it. It comes by itself: a new Black and Decker packed without instructions. Nor will the group one wishes to use it on give any hints. For them money is the one great unmentionable: it has to be, for that is what allows the effortless maintainence which defines each group. Accordingly each group, each cocoon will seem to have a 'secrecy' of its money perfect to keep any of the lower groups out. A middle-class invitee at the Derby will hear murmurings not of the real nitty gritty of what brought the people around him there, nothing of the rules for advancement in banking firms, or lobbying through consultancies and other bribes in government for giant tax dodges on big money, or ways of rigging privileged schools as charities. That is outside – beams and gridwork and other messy supporting stuff. The murmurings that can be overheard are internal, ways of living and references to others' ways of living, maybe references to lubricating the great machine that supports it; but nothing that carries the information about how to make a setting where such murmurings are possible.

A working-class misfit in a middle-class gathering will also be befuddled, hearing murmurings not of mortgage tax relief or details of university entrance coaching and other things that could get him there behind the hand happily pouring the drinks; only chatter of the life inside what those necessities have produced.

To this privacy, this closing off of knowledge, there is only one exception: a blurter, a gusher, a happy spiller of all that is most important to hold secret. This is the man who has just arrived. With his big mouth and attempt to make clear everything needed to get where he is, he holds open the cocoon to other outsiders. He also brings the walls caving down on those already inside, by his words and precision and too-clearly money-obsessed actions that let what should be the invisible world of the outside supporting framework inside, into the center, where no one in the cocoon can escape it clacking and crunching around them. He is the *nouveau riche*, and in a country where the eternal battle of invisible money rages, where the anti-democratic ideal of private knowledge and secret ways-in dominates, he will be hated with a universality that is, indeed, one of the sole bonds across the land.

Where he will be accepted is in the United States. This is the country where the once Mrs. John De Lorean could have a pillow embroidered with the slogan,

BETTER NOUVEAU RICHE THAN NEVER RICHE AT ALL

and the magazines that reported it could, with hardly any exceptions, remark on her honesty with pride. There is a good reason for this. You can only have a category boundary problem, the revulsion at seeing a creature which is neither fish nor fowl, if you have the notion of closed-up, immutable categories to begin with. Those, in the social realm, will be the cocoons and bubbles of English delight, but in America they will, generally, not be there strongly enough for the upset to exist. Stroll through the living rooms of some of the stateliest homes around Louisville before the Kentucky Derby and you will find people talking about money: powerfully, insistently, in clear voices, trying to make all details clear, interrupting each other even louder when a mistake on investment advice has been made and needs to be corrected with more figures, more details, more detailed lore of money. There are exceptions, of course, some old money individuals who have fully accepted the English model, but the ideal is clarity, universal admission, and no shame at all about this beautiful, all-purchasing tool of money.

It is an honesty appropriate to a country built on technology, and populated by immigrants. Technology is clear, as money is clear. How could you have steam locomotives or the Winchester repeating rifle or the Apple Macintosh computer if all you ever revealed about them were polite murmurs, unspecific and with embarrassment at details? One would not wish to travel over a bridge built by engineers who communicated only with such detail-lacking politesse. What you need instead are blueprints, technical specifications, exact language, nothing barred. Such clarity is also just what lots of ambitious immigrants would want to have around as the dominant ethos: for only with such clear and so reproducible rules could they hope to move up. Whether any one of these aspects was prior is probably not worth trying to decide. What counts is that blueprint-sharp clarity in technology, styles of living, and the use of money can easily support each other, and in the United States have come to do so. A resident of that country who is going to bore you with a monotonous recounting of the civic structures in his city is likely to go on with a similar recitation of shopping habits or the prices he has encountered in his recent travels. There is a similarity in this insistent monotone, the recounting of detailed mechanical fact, with that of hi-fi or car or computer buffs from any other country – creatures who tend to be generally pleased with the US, too, it has been noted.

If the *nouveau riche* finds his natural home in America, why then do people go on about him so in Britain? It makes no sense if he is only a sign of a foreign culture. This he is not. The strain on Britons today is that while they have that vivid, immensely desirable model of the warm cocoons all around them, they also, great gobs of them, want to move up, and accept the advancement ideology which says they can and should. All of the American causes operate, perhaps stealthily and in general silence but still with great power, here too. British jobs will just as frequently demand clear and logical thinking, at least in a restricted realm, and as to being immigrants who naturally want to see how the new world thay have landed in works, not only will there have been that general economic prosperity to bring people up, but there will be that biological literalness of immigration at least internally and in class terms. The distance from 1830s rural Lancashire or even 1930s industrial Bradford to 1980s Basingstoke is not more than most families now living in America have experienced over that time. The newly rich individual, his attributes and above all his need for clarity, is there hiding inside British people too. That inner being is keen to get out, or at least to tug the body around him in the direction he wants to make it go. Show an uncouth money-spouting man in the press, television or conversation, and the inner soul will watch in envy, the outer one will watch in revulsion. The result will be the fascination we can only have towards a creature skimming along the dividing line between two divergent worlds, both of which have their pull on us.

Which means that if middle-class England were less of a *nouveau riche* country its inhabitants would be more at ease. As it is, their social agony is that of the acquisitive man throughout time, made worse by the fact that they can't quite admit it or work fully towards that goal. The resistance is not just from the outside, but from inside too: that cocoon ideal, on display throughout society and backed with that metaphysics of eternal satisfaction, is terribly attractive. The result is that the two desires hit, and it's exhausting. The problem is universal, and again is only worth discussing in the British case because of its being especially clear there. The battle of money on the outside – whether you should hold yours, or whether you should try to see the way to get theirs – is mimicked by the battle of clarity inside: whether out of the seething inner world we should pick actions that maintain our current position and confidences, or whether we should try to poke, quibble, assess and otherwise move our way on. It is a macrocosm let within, a miniaturized mechanical *nouveau riche* man inside.

Simply holding the body, let alone opening the mouth, becomes a difficult thing to do. Everything is tense, brittle, caught between the two possibilities. It is much more interesting than the tension and uncertainties of simple social climbing, for it will be reproduced in every part of life. It is delectably clear in the magnificent Basil Fawlty comic character, continually tempted, yet continually holding back what his assessment suggests, quivering and tensing from the repression, until finally, through chance or the consequences of his restraint earlier on, he lets loose, not wildly but in rigid, precise forms that just happen to be the reverse of what his discretion earlier would have insisted upon. He is a spy continually blowing his cover – whence the fascinated tension in watching Alec Guinness showing Smiley get it just right, too.

As a useful side-effect this Basil Fawlty-like tenseness can, when felt deeply enough, keep the social system in harmony. Every person will accept the fairness or at least the usualness of being assessed by those around him. Even standing on a street corner an Englishman will often appear to be on patrol, tense and not relaxed, for the stability of the whole rests on his being ready to display himself, and to assess everyone else, not for how they are dressed – that's trivial, a matter of individual baubles – but for how they fit in that social whole. It's a far cry from the posture of ordinary Americans, who are quite content to let the whole take care of itself, since they, almost by definition, are the whole, that being built up of ordinary people. In Britain, accordingly, classes get divided up into meticulously ordered sub-classes, and in his mauling battle of all against all there is little time to question what the commanders of the operation are doing, back behind the lines, in their commandeered chateaux with wine and white linen tablecloths. It will be easy to accept the fact that people with much power will not need to justify themselves or even make themselves clear; indeed, there will be delight when powerful people make a point of pretending not to know things, since by doing so they reiterate the cozy ease of that niche up there which we all would like. It might be aristocrats with their mannered bumbling; it might be sports stars who say 'It just comes natural'. In both events it is pure 'being', unfettered and with no need of improvement: and in so much as that's our ideal, who could wish to say it is wrong? To respect a lack of questioning, elegantly solves the social harmony problem by not even letting it get started – since no one would wish to disgrace himself by posing it. This is social cement as strong as it comes.

III.   Back now to the *Sunday Times*, where the eternal battle of money and open vs closed knowledge is written so clear. For fourteen years, starting in 1967, the *Sunday Times* was edited by one man, and in that time it developed a style, a tone, a consistent attitude on how to face the world, that was just right for these problems of the middle- and upper-middle-class Englishman. There was the Insight team, to show how with logic and persistent questioning one can enter into any number of otherwise apparently closed-tight worlds. There was the insistent personalizing and psychological dramatization of large, complex stories, to show how even for people on the inside of important bubbles – in the Treasury, at the Newmarket sales – life was not entirely protected, but that there always was some awareness of what was maintaining them, of those external supporting girders clanking away. And there was also that famous color supplement magazine, where the mix of ads for new consumer goods alongside articles urging compassion for poor or starving people was not grating, since both came from a spirit of generosity towards people who hoped to make themselves anew and strive upwards. The paper sold, was respected, attracted many of the best journalists in Britain, and sold even more.

   How much did it have to be this way? To this question there is no general answer. The backing patterns we've suggested are ones that had to work on a level of abstraction just one step too high – they were about the chosen setting of the soul, not the doings of that soul once the choice was made – to be precise enough to give specific solutions. It was a backing that guided, tracked, and constrained thoughts, but could not create them. Thus although the Insight team often used only trivial cases to show the power of rational investigation to batter into closed realms – picture fakers, wine mis-labellers, and other disturbers of the goods of delicate social transaction – they also sometimes turned their technique to more important worlds: corrupt plane manufacturers, selfish phar-maceutical giants, and the like. Either choice would have been consistent with the most general English middle-class attitudes. Nothing in the attitudes alone could have predicted one or the other. Particulars cannot come from generalities, unless you add in some more particulars to direct how they will be used. The occasional choice of DC-10s rather than Burgundy labels came because Harold Evans and his best writers were plucky men.

The more interesting question comes from trying to reverse our reasoning, and seeing what happens to the underlying ideas when they're put in a new setting, different from the one that got them started. To a certain point they will stretch and twist to try to wrap around the new setting, while beyond that point they will snap. But can we specify those twistings, and the point at which that snap comes? Luckily the current *Sunday Times* allows us to do just that. This is because after the years of the Evans consensus the paper was taken over by Rupert Murdoch, in 1981, and once the necessary properties were over, he brought in new men whose job was to change it. They did pretty much what Thatcher was trying to do to the whole country. What was the new *Sunday Times* setting, and what did the readers make of it?

Some of the new setting was just fussy details. Murdoch was in the middle of a deal to broadcast television by satellite into English homes when be bought the paper, and quite naturally wanted to use it to help make that deal work. The necessary financial journalists started writing about the wonders of free competition in the satellite broadcast market, and also about the need to put ads on the BBC (which would make it a weaker competitor to a future satellite system).

That tactical bias was easy for readers to adjust to. Satellite TV can easily be seen as good because new things are good, 'just made' like the shallowly rooted readers themselves; laws against ads on the BBC are worth dropping because external constraints against anyone's life are bad, readers as well as the very rich. That's simple fairness, openness, and the ability to move on.

A bigger Murdoch change was the attack on unions. Partly this was because Murdoch himself hated unions since they got in his way and he doesn't like anything that gets in his way; partly it was because he was a keen supporter of Thatcher, and her administration was predicated upon a hate of unions, for class support and other reasons. In any event he gave the orders; the new men, plus many individuals who had stayed on the staff from the previous era and saw which way advancement lay, through the key news and commissioning feature editors got to work. Soon they had changed the terrain of the paper considerably from the Evans days, when industrial unions appeared in the columns sometimes as good things, and sometimes as bad. In the Murdoch paper, even three or four years before Murdoch fired all his unionized printers and moved to Wapping, they became never good: many articles made sense only if you assumed that they cheated, lied, destroyed Britain, were run by maniacs, murdered people, and that you had to be near-retarded to be in one.

In a simpler paper it would have been enough to leave this at a level of slogan and imperative. In the *Sunday Times*, though, where readers were used to argument or at least lengthy backing of positions, something more was needed. But what could it be? The more tolerant approach in the Evans years had after all been consistent with middle-class British beliefs. How could their beliefs cover this opposite?

The solution of the *Sunday Times* journalists is illuminating. Without instruction, without the need for memos or directives or pep-talks from imported media consultants, they began to emphasize just one aspect of the underlying attitude and show that it would be destroyed by unions. It couldn't be that unions would violate our ideal of staying in a warm cocoon – unions after all were known for supporting their members. Rather it had to be an overemphasis on the other ideal they would hinder, that of emerging out and clambering forward, escaping from the past and all its grasping bonds. The paper began to describe unions as having The Wrong attitude to history. They were caught in history, they were immersed in and left over from history, they were big sloshing monsters from the sticky mud of the past. There is no free movement if you're stuck to history, and a life without free movement is horrid, locking in the social arrangements you're temporarily at. History is something you're supposed to leap-frog along in, so it needs gaps, holes, loose spots – not a heavy, sludging continuously squelchy grip.

The technique used in carrying this out was to accuse unions and their supporters of being old. There had always been something of that in the paper, but now it pervaded. Sometimes in the Murdoch paper they were merely doddering:

> **It is a change that the Labour Party, muttering about . . . has yet to grasp.**
>
> (magazine, April 14, 1985, p. 34).

while sometimes they were even older than that, biological curios:

> **organised with all the intricacy of a medieval craft guild.**
>
> (ibid., p. 42)

In all cases nothing could make them change, as they forever 'clung' to their restrictive practices, their overmanning, and anything else out of the past. If they were modern it was an occasion for mirth:

> **The Labour party has entered the plastic card age at last. You can now order party publications . . . quoting any of the four major credit cards.**
>
> (Atticus, April 21, 1985, p. 16)

Indeed, the only positive reference I could find to industrial unions in a long search in the Murdoch paper, going back well before the move to Wapping, was a photo-spread on mementoes of the early unions, presented as delightful historical trinkets, like Victorian coffee urns. Certainly that couldn't be of any practical use to us. If the unions tried to grapple with our problems it would be impulsively, passionately, and with big dripping bits of the past still sticking on to them afterwards; not coolly, calmly, and with clean hands as one should.

Where have we heard this before? It is the writings of H.G.Wells, of course, the past of coarse war-lords, slavering often hairy kings, and other unpleasant Darwinian precursors. We, who have discovered science and the scientific approach to social organization – all new, clean, fresh – can be freed from them and the rest of the past. The reason Wells is not taken seriously today is that he was wrong – science and scientific organization are what brought us the Somme, fire-storms, etc. The past is not so easily discarded. But who wants to be reminded of that? Certainly not Wells; he was getting enough grief from the circle his wealth put him in because of his past as a draper's apprentice, and his family that had been in service. And certainly not the *Sunday Times* reader either, Wells's class brother under the skin. Unions came from the past, and from the lower classes; that is to say, unions came from something which is biologically within almost all middle-class Englishmen today. They are again our distorted cousins. Who wants to welcome them back home? Presented with a focus on sludgy history, that's the only choice the *Sunday Times* reader gets.

Readers could easily stretch their underlying attitudes to match this protection of free movement in history. It was, after all, something that was already there, and only had to be tugged out a little bit more to one side than usual. That was what had made it easy for the journalists too. The technique of rousing protective emotion through isolating and threatening just one aspect of the underlying ideas is a powerful one, and what journalists who understood their readership would naturally tend to do when the time came to switch the trend of articles in the direction the new boss wanted.

So along with the tugging that aroused fears of being heaved out of history's interesting flow and sequestered in the backwater of one's original cocoon, we might expect that the new *Sunday Times* would also begin to present articles that tugged disproportionately in the other direction. This it did. What if one would never be allowed to return to the cocoon, and all was flux, hurry and rush? That would be terrible too. This reverse tug was necessary for a very large category of news articles Murdoch wished to present. They weren't on specific topics, like the union ones, but rather had a tone that Murdoch wanted to push. Those who know Mr. Murdoch say that he has ideas he likes and ideas he hates, and that he thinks it's a lot of pommy weakness to go on about them once a sensible guy has made up his mind. Means might be open to discussion and refinement – that's only good business practice – but not ends. Accordingly all his political hates and loves – roughly the Thatcherite or Reagan consensus – had to be presented as having no other side. He would not like a paper of his to do otherwise. It would be wrong. It would be ridiculous. It would be giving aid to the enemy. And Murdoch does not like to be wrong, or ridiculous, and he never, ever, gives aid to his enemies.

Again it would have been easy in a simple paper – you just present one side to every issue and that's that – but *Sunday Times* readers expected more. What the journalists began to do accordingly was to introduce a sort of 'bracketing' in their presentation of each news article that had any political importance. Both sides would get a chance to be presented, but the wrong side would be bracketed both fore and aft by the correct side. This would not just happen typographically, but in the even more basic point of who is allowed to present ideas. Thus in a magazine article on the Nicaraguan Contras (April 21, 1985) readers were carefully told not to listen to what the Sandinistas said, even if, as the article also noted, it happened to be true. When Ortega says that

The US is 'just a step away from declaring war'

we should pay no attention to it, for

that is a familiar refrain in Managua.

What we should pay attention to is the fact that

the bellicose noises from Washington are causing genuine concern among America's allies.

The bad guys are devalued even as they're quoted. It was the same in reporting the all-party reflationary proposal that year called the 'Charter for Jobs' in terms of Thatcher's scornful response: it was 'challenged' and 'dismissed' for eight paragraphs before being briefly described – with its supporters being referred to not directly but only as instances of something that was 'worrying ministers' (April 21, 1985, p. 1). If the *Sunday Times* turned anti-Thatcher, for tactical purposes to forestall the Labour Party or other reasons, it would no doubt be in the same question-suppressing way.

This sounds unreasonable all bare and summarized here, but think what it's like to read this stuff, coming across it in that leisured browse through the pages. The removal of extraneous news sources has let its readers escape from the flux! Choice, worry and all the problems of alternatives in a busy outside world are banished – a break that, every now and then, is relaxing for us all to get. Think too what this makes of anyone who disagrees with the government, or supports Ortega, or otherwise goes against the paper's insistent line. They are brutes, who would tear us from our cocoons and dump us in the flux. They are ontological muggers. The only protection will be to steady the head, concentrate the eyes, and stick to the straight and narrow, the paper's one true interpretation.

What is it like for the poor *Sunday Times* reader to be tugged and pulled this way, now threatened with being dumped in the flux, now (remember the unions) with being locked away from it forever? The paper's circulation figures are only a little help. Some readers seem to have left and gone to the *Observer*, where a tone close to that of the Evans years at the *Sunday Times* still prevails. But almost all stayed, and have even been joined by some new ones. What they think is speculation, but still worth a try. Possibly some do not notice the changes: there is, after all, a great core of the old paper which remains. Possibly some do see the contrary backings to the arguments that are being pushed, but are not that worried about contradiction, expecially as the paper's harshness of tone matches the harsh economy so well. Maybe even some enjoy the passion brought out when the bases of their thought are touched and poked at so daringly. Whatever, I suspect that the feel of reading it is different from the feel of reading the old paper, since it is based on the old ideas but with them now somehow pulled wider, so that to match them the reader has to let the constituent parts of his personality be tugged at least a little bit in different directions too.

The big question comes in the third main change Murdoch has made. This is the lauding of businessmen. Powerful international executives are good, but even small-scale property developers or just factory-running entrepreneurs will do. There are descriptions in his paper of their homes, their offices, their bright ideas, and, especially, their hunt for money, money, money. This is nice – who's against money? – but the problem is that in the pages of the *Sunday Times* these businessmen never *stop* in their hunt. They are ever busy, ever ready. And by now we know what such ceaseless action means. Such entrepreneurs destroy the premise of arriving at a state which would fit in a 'Life in the Day of' feature. They are stuck on a Buddhist-like infinite wheel of suffering instead, constantly striving, never at ease. All they can do is make money, which by the essence of the traditional *Sunday Times* and the mix of personality ideals that backed it, is a means and not an end.

Will the current readers take it? The question is the same as asking what they will make of Thatcher's pushing of entrepreneurs. It's a bigger change than union-bashing or news bracketing. Accept the individual businessman ideal, and the tautened ideas are finally stretched too far. They snap. One side, life permanently outside the cocoon, wins out. There is no space for coziness or relaxation; no space really for even spending indulgent long hours in a lounge chair, in front of the fire, with that cup of tea and your favourite slippers on, poking through a paper that makes you feel good. The reader would have to leap up, stride into action, and leave the crumpled paper on the floor behind, in the warm room, only perhaps a smiling photo of the Queen on page one left to show what had been.

When the British reader does that, Murdoch's personality transfer will have become complete. But I somehow doubt if it will happen soon. An American can get up and stride out, for he knows what's beyond the room door: it is the future, which beckons him and tells him it is right to go. But in Britain? Beyond the room doors are just some dark and draughty corridors, or God knows perhaps even the man's family. His world depends on staying still and in the right place except when travelling directly towards another still and right place. That is in his acts and thoughts and friends' expectation, and even in his rarely explicit but still insistently murmuring view of immortality. So let's leave the man where he closes the paper, and drops it on the floor, front page up, Queen still smiling. Let's leave him there, warming in front of the fire, not getting up and leaving the good room. Who would want to convince him that he should?